THE STORYBOOK OF OPERA

Volume II

The dramas of: Tosca, The Elixir of Love, Tristan
und Isolde, Rigoletto, Il Trovatore, The Magic Flute,
Hansel und Gretel

by
Cyrus Henry Biscardi

Foreword by Ann Blyth

Illustrations by Kitty Chang

LP LEARNING PUBLICATIONS, INC.
Holmes Beach, Florida

Library of Congress Cataloging-in-Publication Data

(Revised for vol. 2)

Biscardi, Cyrus Henry
  The Storybook of Opera

  Includes bibliographies and indexes.
  Summary: Presents the stories of Tosca, The Elixir of
Love, Tristan und Isolde, and four other operas.
  Also includes a list of American and international opera
companies and a glossary of operatic terms.
  1. Operas—Stories, plots, etc.—Juvenile literature.
2. Opera—Juvenile literature. [1. Operas—Stories, plots,
etc. 2. Opera] I. Title.
MT95.B57 1987 782.1'3 86-81155
  ISBN 0-918452-99-6

Learning Publications, Inc.
Box 1326, 5351 Gulf Drive
Holmes Beach, Florida 34217-1326

Illustrations by Kitty Chang

Printing: 1 2 3 4 5 6 7 8 9   Year: 7 8 9 0 1 2

DEDICATION

To Ann Blyth, singer-actress, star of screen, stage, television—a gracious lady and dear friend.

CONTENTS

Contents of Volume I, *The Storybook of Opera*:
   Die Fledermaus (The Bat), Romeo et Juliette, Il Barbiere di Siviglia (The Barber of Seville),
Carmen, La Forza del Destino (The Force of Destiny), La Traviata (The Lost One), La Boheme
(The Bohemian Girl) and Madama Butterfly. Foreword by Franco Corelli.

FOREWORD

I'm sure that readers will find (as I did) that this *Storybook* is really a panoramic view of the world of opera, written in a style that carried me, and will carry them, along a road of high adventure and remarkable beauty.

I especially enjoyed how the reader is literally taken into the house and given a description of the setting, including the last dimming of the lights, just before this fantasy world opens before one's eyes. Every adult who lets his or her heart open to this experience inevitably has a child-like fascination about it.

I also greatly appreciated reading accurate translations rather than the insipid summaries I've read in the past. What a different view of *Tosca* one gets when one understands exactly what she says in her encounter with Scarpia, and later in her touching final scene with her beloved. Needless to say, for me personally, *all* the stories brought back a flood of fond memories.

Finishing both volumes was like getting off a magic carpet that had taken me all over the world. And I believe that readers will particularly appreciate the sensitive way pertinent personal and historic facts about the composers and their times are presented. All in all, the well-named *Storybook of Opera* is a study long overdue, and one that should give great pleasure for years to come.

Ann Blyth

PREFACE

Through years of radio, and through more and more telecasts, the audience for opera has grown, and continues to grow, into many millions. And libretto translations and synopsis attempts simply do not fill the need for *accurate*, dramatic and easily read stories that bring to life the characters and the music.

I remember my reaction to opera when I saw my first performance of *La Boheme* at a very early age. I came away with a good feeling about the music; but the thing that stood out was the comedy in the garret and the French loaves of bread. As with newcomers today, I needed to know more.

So to help create a real interest in the rewarding world of opera for readers of all ages (and perhaps a new insight for opera buffs), I have brought to them these "stories with music" in an entirely different and informative way.

The Storybook of Opera, Volumes I and II, treats the stories the way people are used to reading stories. There are conversations between the characters; there are descriptions of what they look like and where they are located—and, in addition, there are helpful references to the music as each story unfolds.

In each one I have followed exactly what the composer and his writers wanted to say, but where literal translations may not have given the true meaning, the *sense* of the words has been set down for utmost clarity. You'll notice the use of three dots (ellipses) and dashes quite frequently. With these I have tried to give you a feeling of the *music*, too, and how the singers are expressing themselves.

By going directly to the original language, I discovered that translations into English often missed the mark. And if the attempt was made to rhyme the words, then the real meanings were off altogether. (Of course, sometimes an opera plot defies logic, so one must just attribute it to "operatic license" that helps propel the action and perhaps deepen the suspense.)

Regarding the "new toy" of supertitles, a leading music critic commented that "even at best supertitles do not. . .substitute for knowing what the characters are saying, moment to moment." A great part of the thrill of opera is in entering into a "bond" with the artists on stage. Being distracted from this by looking up and away just serves to destroy that oneness with the singer and the drama.

After all, the magic of a performance ultimately depends on the quality of the singers, and the ability of the conductor. To have a singer move an audience to leap to its feet, calling "bravos" at every chance, cheering and clapping in pure joy, is an unforgettable experience. And the artist who could accomplish that again and again is the one who wrote the foreword for Volume I, Franco Corelli. He weaved that magic through his magnetic presence and his sensitive interpretations—a singer whose heart was in his voice.

And, in dedicating this second volume to a singer-actress of world fame, I'm reminded of her equally memorable performances on film. Ann Blyth's special beauty matched the warm beauty of her voice as she gave us the Princess in *Kismet* ("Baubles, Bangles and Beads") and the unhappy lover left behind by *The Student Prince* (Mario Lanza). On stage tours (*Sound of Music, Kiss Me Kate, The Merry Widow*) and on television, parts both musical and dramatic. It is indeed gratifying to have her foreword to Volume II express her enjoyment of this work.

I am hopeful that *Storybook* will help introduce you to other wonderful artists as it brings you "a new way to enter and appreciate a most fascinating, fulfilling and emotional Wonderland."

ACKNOWLEDGEMENTS

Out of quite a few, there are some especially whom I would like to thank. The envelope please:

Marion and Don Rahman who introduced me to a certain important celebrity. Oscar Muller, overseer of what I translated from the German, and other things. John Castellana for witnessing the deed. Paul Zangas, artistic specifier. My brother Jeff, for his professional handling of the covers. My daughter Denise, for valuable young-person opinions. Kitty Chang for her "no problem" attitude. Roslyn's William Cullen Bryant Library staffers who found the references I needed. Dr. Edsel Erickson, Publisher, for his enthusiasm and warmth, and his most capable and understanding staff. And to Mrs. Corelli for her gracious help and thoughtfulness.

And through it all, the encouragement, the love, the resolve of my dear wife Dorothy who typed and retyped the manuscript until it seemed it would never end. Thanks.

Introduction

You will remember in Volume I traveling with Giacomo Puccini from the Latin Quarter of Paris (*La Boheme*) to the strange and beautiful islands of Japan (*Madama Butterfly*). On the one hand, Mimi was a girl Rodolfo loved above everything else even though she would leave him to try to find a better life. On the other, Butterfly was abandoned after only one night of love—and left to die by her own hand. In both places we enjoyed the kind of lovely lyrical music that made Puccini so famous.

But he had made another stop in between. And he had changed his music to fit the dramatic, evil and brooding Rome of 1800. Of course, the Puccini magic was still there, but it was now colored by powerful melodrama.

Once again, his heroine was based on a true person—a famous singer-actress of strong emotions—jealous, loving, scheming, violent. He had met her in Paris through the play written by France's most popular playwright of that time—Victorien Sardau. But he wasn't sure that she was his kind of girl

After all, his earlier women, Manon and Mimi, "were different from Tosca," he told Sardau. To which the Frenchman replied, "Women in love all belong to the same family!" Sardau also knew that his play was made great mostly because the great Sarah Bernhardt was its star. He therefore gave Puccini very little trouble when his five acts were made into three.

The blood-and-thunder action takes place in three locations still to be seen today in Rome-the Eternal City. It is June. There is war—and revolution. There has been news that Napoleon has been defeated in battle with the Austrians who rule Italy. And as the curtain rises we are in the magnificent Church of Sant' Andrea della Valle. Three violent chords...then drums...and one final threatening chord, prepare us for the grim, dark action that will take place...as we begin....

1

TOSCA

ACT I

The huge church is empty. On the right are iron gates that close off the chapel of the Attavanti family. On the left is a wooden platform in front of a large painting covered with a white cloth. Whoever the painter is, he has not yet arrived. A dim light filters down showing the statue of the Madonna on a pedestal and a basin for holy water.

Suddenly, a ragged figure rushes in. It's Cesare Angelotti (CHEH-sah-reh Ahn-gel-UH-tee) who was consul of the "Roman Republic" before he was thrown into prison for being on the side of the French. He is frantically looking for a key that was supposed to be hidden by his sister at the bottom of the statue. He finds it! He swiftly goes to the little chapel, opens the gates, and disappears inside.

He's no sooner hidden than we hear the violins start a light, cheery tune. They introduce the Sacristan (in charge of the sacred things) mumbling and grumbling to himself. (Remember Friar Melitone in Verdi's *Forza*?) He's holding a bunch of painter's brushes.

> "Always washing! And every brush is dirtier than a kid's collar!"

When he turns to the scaffold (the painter's platform) he's surprised to see that the artist isn't there. He could have sworn that the Cavalier Cavaradossi had come back! (Had he heard Angelotti?) But when he climbs up the steps and looks into the food basket he's convinced that no one had arrived.

The sound of three bells announces the Angelus...the call to prayer. The Sacristan kneels quickly and prays softly. And from a side door the artist finally comes in.

After asking the caretaker what he is doing, he climbs up to the painting and takes away the cloth that is covering it.

> "It's her picture!" exclaims the Sacristan.

> "Whose?"

> "That unknown girl who has been praying here these past days..."

Yes, Cavaradossi had seen her and since she was praying so hard he was able to catch her lovely face without her knowing it. The grumbler thinks it's the work of Satan, the devil!

But Mario Cavaradossi (MAH-ree-oh Cah-vah-rah-DUH-see) pays no attention and asks him to hand over his paints. He quickly begins, while the sacristan comes and goes, bringing in a bowl so he can still clean the brushes. Suddenly Mario stops. From his pocket he takes out a small picture of his lady love, Floria Tosca (FLUH-ree-ah TUH-sca). He looks up at the painting of the blond, blue-eyed Mary Magdalene and then back at the portrait of Tosca.

Here the composer gives Cavaradossi a most beautiful aria— and one of the most important in the opera. It starts off with a big word: "Re-CON-dita." In English the word is spelled almost the same: "RE-con-dite." And according to the dictionary it means "beyond the ability of someone to understand; deep, hidden, mysterious."

The artist has seen the mysterious harmony between two women who look so different, yet can be so much alike inside. There is a "hidden harmony" (Recondita armonia) that the mystery of art can mix together. . . and although he is painting a blond beauty. . . "my only thought—Tosca, is of you!"

Mary Magdalene of the Bible was a "fallen woman" who was saved by a higher love. And Floria Tosca (as we shall see later on) was almost conquered until her inner strength, her passion for Mario, gave her the power to do something she never thought she could!

Throughout this wonderful song, we can hear old mumble, grumble complaining about the saints being neglected.

"These different women. . . are sinners—all of them! Instead, let's make the Sign of the Cross. . . "

Now he wants to leave. That's all right with Mario. Then he sees the food basket still full. Isn't the artist hungry—or is he trying to have his sins forgiven? When Cavaradossi tells him he really isn't hungry, the Sacristan looks at the food with appetite— but then puts it aside and finally goes.

Mario continues to paint. His back is to the Attavanti (Ah-tah-VAHN-tee) Chapel. But when Angelotti (who doesn't see the painter) turns the key in the lock to get out, Mario hears him! He turns to see who it is.

For one dreadful moment, Angelotti, seeing the movement, thinks he's been found. . . but then he recognizes his old friend Cavaradossi! Doesn't the artist know him? Has prison changed him so much? But no, Mario does remember—and they clasp each other's arms.

"I have just run away from the Castel Sant'Angelo."

"Tell me what I can do," declares Mario.

Before the escaped man can answer, a voice from a distance calls Mario! It's Tosca! A jealous woman! Mario will send her away in a moment.

"Here I am," calls the artist, patiently.

Angelotti is faint with hunger! Grabbing the basket of food, Mario pushes him back into the chapel.

"Mario! Mario! Mario!"

"I'm here...," sings Mario as he unlocks the door.

Tosca's gentle, flowing musical theme (that we will hear again and again) begins. She rushes in. She refuses Mario's kiss, and looks here and there.

"Why was it locked?" she asks suspiciously.

"That's what the Sacristan wanted."

"Who were you talking to?"

"To you!"

But Tosca is not to be fooled. Mario *was* whispering to someone—"where is she?" When Mario asks her who she is talking about, Tosca insists that it was a woman because she heard the rustle of her dress!

The violins take up a sweet melody as Mario denies that there was anyone else and tries to kiss his loved one. At last, Tosca feels that maybe there wasn't another woman—but she coyly moves away from his kiss saying, "In front of the Madonna...!" No, she first wants to pray and place some flowers around the statue.

So Mario laughingly goes back to his painting. In a few moments, Tosca has ended her prayer and turns to her lover.

"Now listen to me: I am singing tonight, but it's a short program. You will wait for me at the stage exit, and to your villa we'll go alone...all alone."

This now causes a big problem for Mario. Tonight, of all nights! He's got his friend to worry about. But Tosca (in a light, heavenly voice) is dreamily thinking of having her lover all to herself. The moon will be full and the flowers will fill the air with their perfume. Isn't he happy? She starts to wonder.

"A lot," sings Mario, without too much thought.

"Say it again!"

"A lot."

"You say it badly..."

Tosca sits next to him on the steps. She begins a sensitive aria which Mario soon joins. It is the famous love duet. She reminds him of the "little house" that is theirs alone...hidden among the plants. She describes how wonderful it is to be there away from it all...listening to the sounds of the night that "whisper about tiny loves...as the moon shines down on fields of flowers and the sea winds blow!" Tosca is full of love for Mario. He can no longer resist her. He is captured by this "siren." Their voices climb together. Mario promises to be with her. (But he still has to take care of his friend.) He wants Tosca to leave so that he can "work." And although she tells him that she is going, she glances up at the painting.

"Who is that blonde woman up there?"

"Magdalene. Like her?"

"She's too beautiful!"

As she looks closer she begins to see someone she knows. She's seen those sky-blue eyes before. Suddenly, she recognizes her—it's the young Attavanti! Tosca is blind with jealousy. Does he meet with her? Does she love him? Does he love her?

Mario tries to calm her down. He explains that he just saw the girl yesterday by chance...that she comes to pray...and that he painted her without her knowing it.

"Swear!"

"I swear!"

Tosca now believes that the figure is staring at her...laughing at her. Mario thinks that's foolishness, and in a sweeping melody he sings to her lovely eyes so dark and flashing...so soft with love—no other eyes in the world can compare with her black eyes!

This does it. Tosca melts at his words...yet she still asks him to "change the girl's eyes to black!" Cavaradossi can't help teasing her about her jealousy. He insists that he loves only her...while she tells him that he would change the eyes if he knew how much it meant to her! As his voice rises to a thrilling high note, Cavaradossi speaks of her "bold anger...and her throbbing love!" Tosca wants to hear more.

"I shall always say, 'Floria, I love you!'"

Cavaradossi now really wants her to leave. Will he stay faithful to her? He swears to it again, as he tries to hurry her out. She notices this and her jealousy begins to rise once more.

"Still?"

"No, forgive me!" says Tosca as she falls into his arms for a kiss.

But Mario, using the same words that *she* did when he wanted to kiss *her*, says jokingly, "In front of the Madonna?" With a little smile, Tosca looks up at him and once again begs him to make the eyes black! And with that he kisses her and she hurries away.

Now for Angelotti. Mario waits until Tosca's footsteps fade. Then he quickly meets his friend at the gates of the chapel. What to do? Hide in Rome or get away? To his surprise, the girl whom Mario has been painting is Angelotti's sister. She has left him some of her own clothes as a disguise! Mario sees that it was a sister's love and not a lover's meeting place that brought the girl to church so often.

"Now I understand!"

"She has done everything to keep me out of the clutches of that scoundrel, Scarpia (SKAHR-pee-ah)!"

"Scarpia?"

Mario is furious at that smutty hypocrite!

"It may cost me my life, but I'll save you!"

It isn't safe to stay till dark, yet Angelotti fears the daylight. However, the chapel opens out on to some woods and a path that leads right to Mario's villa! He gives him the key and advises Angelotti to take along the woman's costume. Mario will join him before nightfall. There's no need to put the clothes on now since the path will be deserted.

Then, just as Angelotti is about to rush away, Mario remembers the well. At the first sign of danger he must get to the well. Halfway down is a narrow pass that leads to a dark space. There he will find a safe hiding-place!

The words are hardly out of Mario's mouth when there is the sound of a cannon. It is the signal that someone has escaped! They hear somebody coming! Without another look around they both flee through the chapel.

In runs the Sacristan! He's got great news for Cavaradossi or anyone else. What's this? He's gone! Before the Sacristan can get over his disappointment, the whole church fills up with priests, students and the boys' choir. They come in from all over.

"What's happened?"

"Haven't you heard? Bonaparte...the scoundrel..."

He goes on to tell them that Napoleon has been defeated! That night there will be a torch parade and a party at the Farnese Palace where Floria Tosca is going to sing! He brushes them along to get dressed.

"Go to the sacristy!"

Of course the children's choir loves the whole idea. They laugh and shout as they think of their "double pay!"

"Te Deum! Gloria! Long live the king! We'll celebrate the victory!"

But their joy quickly comes to an end. To the sound of deep, heavy notes we hear the voice of the hated Scarpia! He strides in with his spy Spoletta and some other policemen.

"Such an uproar—in church! A fine respect!"

The Sacristan is shaking with fear. He tries to explain. But Scarpia commands him to get ready for the *Te Deum* (a special church prayer that the choir sings). Then he orders him to stay right where he is. He turns to Spoletta. He is to search every nook and cranny. He orders the others to watch all the doors without being suspected.

"And now for you," he says to the quivering Sacristan.

"Be careful how you answer. A state prisoner has just escaped from the Castel Sant'Angelo. He took refuge here."

The Sacristan is overcome. Scarpia wants to know where the chapel of the Attavanti family is. When they go to it, they find that it is open—and there's a key in the lock!. They both go in. When they get back Scarpia is baffled. He knows that it was a bad mistake to shoot off the cannon. That just helped his prisoner run away. But he has found a "precious clue"! A fan! He wonders who helped Angelotti escape. As he looks over the fan he suddenly spies the coat of arms! It's the crest of Attavanti!

How does it all fit in? He looks suspiciously around, missing nothing. His eyes search the platform and then finally they focus on the painting. It's the Marchesa Attavanti! What does this mean—her fan, her picture?

"Who painted that picture?"

"The Cavalier Cavaradossi..."

Well, this really means something to Scarpia. It is Tosca's lover...Tosca, the one he, Scarpia, wants for himself. His mind begins to see many things. (How to get rid of Cavaradossi is one of them). The basket of food is found—but it's empty. In the chapel full, now empty! And it belongs to the artist. So now all is clear. Mario, the revolutionary, helped the other revolutionary to get food and to escape.

The music picks up Tosca's theme. She enters hurriedly.

"Tosca? She must not see me . . ."

Scarpia hides. He thinks of the fan. He'll use the fan to make Tosca jealous (just as Iago tormented Shakespeare's Othello with the lace handkerchief)!

"Mario! Mario!" calls Tosca.

She's surprised to find him gone. Has he been fooling her? Is he really meeting another? The Sacristan slips away.

This gives Scarpia his chance. He goes to the holy water, wets his fingers and offers Tosca a few drops. She takes them, crosses herself and thanks him. The bells ring again to call the people. By now there is quite a crowd.

Scarpia gets to work. Pure women like Tosca are so rare . . . not like some others who look and dress like Magdalene—but really come to church to plot their love-life. This sets Tosca off. What? What proof . . . what proof?

"Is this what a painter uses?" he asks slyly, showing her the fan. Where was it? On the scaffold. The lovers must have been surprised and the girl rushed away and forgot her fan! Tosca is beside herself. She looks over the fan. There is the crest of Attavanti! She can hardly hold back her tears. She had come to tell Mario that she couldn't meet him after all since she was going to be stuck at the royal celebration. To himself Scarpia is pleased to see the "poison working." Of course, the oily Scarpia is all sympathy. He would love to dry her tears. But Tosca is only thinking of her lover in someone else's arms. This makes Scarpia even happier at seeing the poison of jealousy really taking hold.

Tosca wonders where they are. The traitor! In his villa? She'll crash in on them all of a sudden. She looks up at the portrait.

"You won't have him tonight! I swear!"

Scarpia fakes great surprise . . . *she* swearing in *church*! Tosca's musical theme is heard. Sadly it rises, then softly ends.

"God pardons me. He can see that I'm crying."

She rushes out. The church bells ring again.

Scarpia goes into action. He tells Spoletta to take three men and follow Tosca wherever she goes. They will meet later at the Farnese Palace, Scarpia's headquarters. He sings out his evil desires.

"Go, Tosca! Scarpia will now nest in your heart!"

The drums thunder. Her jealousy will get her to do what he wants. He kneels in prayer as a Cardinal passes by. Meanwhile, the chorus is singing the religious hymn *Te Deum*. But his mind is not on prayer, it's on his passion for Tosca. For her lover— the rope around his neck. As for her—"my arms!" Suddenly he realizes what he has been saying and where he is. He makes the Sign of the Cross.

"Tosca, you make me forget God!"

And as he joins the chorus, the orchestra crashes its cymbals, the drums roar, and the curtain falls.

ACT II

The ancient Farnese Palace (which can still be visited today) is where Scarpia has his rich apartment—on a top floor. He's all dressed up: powdered wig, white ruffled shirt and high-collared coat. He's been waiting for Tosca. Actually, he expects her to lead him to Angelotti. Through him he can accuse Cavaradossi and so kill two birds at once. He's angry because nothing has happened yet. He looks at his watch and then rings a bell. When Sciarrone (Skee-ah-RONE-eh) comes in he asks about Tosca..."has she come to the Palace yet?" Sciarrone reports that one of the servants has gone to look for her.

(Tosca is scheduled to sing at the celebration of Napoleon's defeat. The news had come in that general Melas, head of the Austrian army, had won a great victory. So the Queen of Naples, Maria-Carolina, who wanted to declare war on France, was over-joyed. She is the one throwing the party on a lower floor of the Farnese.)

Scarpia orders his man to open the large window that overlooks the courtyard. The sound of the musicians below comes in through the window. But Tosca has not yet arrived. Although his table is set for supper, he's too occupied to eat.

"Wait for Tosca at the entrance...and tell her I expect to see her after the concert—better yet, give her this note."

Scarpia wants Tosca to come to his quarters so he writes her about Mario's danger. She'll be sure to come to him for love of Mario. (We hear again Tosca's theme.) When Sciarrone leaves, Scarpia reveals himself and shows us what kind of man he really is. He's a sadist. He just wants to get his pleasures wherever he can—the more violent the better—and then throw them aside. He's a cruel, fanatical, lewd and shameless monster who will do anything to get his way. He takes a drink of wine just as Sciarrone comes back to tell him that Spoletta has arrived.

"Well, my good man, how did the hunt go?"

But when Spoletta admits that he followed Tosca to the villa and searched everywhere without finding anything, Scarpia goes into a fit. The trembling Spoletta hears himself condemned to be hanged. He prays under his breath. Then, not knowing what else to say, he mentions that he has taken Cavaradossi! This, of course, pleases Scarpia. He wants him brought in at once. And he also wants the executioner and the judge!

When they have all arrived, Scarpia starts to politely question his victim. Did he know that a prisoner had escaped from the Castle of Sant'Angelo? (They hear Tosca's voice singing at the concert.) Cavaradossi denies everything. Didn't he hide him in the church and give him food and clothing? Lies! The questioning goes on—but Cavaradossi admits nothing.

"He laughed at our questions," reports Spoletta.

"And I'm still laughing!"

This makes Scarpia furious. Meanwhile, the chorus and Tosca's voice have grown so loud that Scarpia angrily shuts the window. He again asks about Angelotti...and the food, the clothes, the villa. And again Mario denies all. Scarpia gets hold of himself and slyly suggests that Cavaradossi could save himself a lot of pain if he would just confess. (The music takes on a mournful sound which will be repeated later.) More questions— but Mario does not give in.

Suddenly, Tosca rushes in. She's stunning in her black gown and flowing cape. She's surprised to see her beloved and runs to kiss him. Mario takes this chance to whisper that she had better not know anything or it will mean his death!

"Mario Cavaradossi...the judge is waiting for your words...," says Scarpia. Then, giving the executioner last minute instructions, Scarpia lets Sciarrone open the door to the torture room and everyone goes in, except Tosca and Scarpia. (The deep, sorrowful music plays, lead by the violins.) She sits on the sofa. She doesn't know that Mario is about to be tortured. Scarpia wants to be friends. He wants to talk nicely as friends should. He doesn't want her to be afraid. When he asks her about the fan she tells him that she was foolish to be jealous and that there was no one at the villa but Mario.

"Yes...*alone!*" repeats Tosca, hitting a high note.

Scarpia wonders if she isn't a little bit *too* sure—maybe she's hiding something. He calls out to the next room. Mario is still denying everything. Well, then, let's "insist"! Tosca laughs that it's useless to try to get anything more. But when Scarpia talks about "a painful hour" if he doesn't get the truth, Tosca is surprised and alarmed. She becomes very excited.

"Oh, God! What's going on? What's going on ?"

Scarpia, with an evil sneer, describes how her lover is tied hand and foot...an iron band around his head...and every time he tells them nothing...the hooks on the band make him bleed!

Tosca can't believe it! But then she hears Mario groan. She begs for pity from "the leering devil." Scarpia now gets around to what he *really* wants!

"It's up to you to save him."

"All right, but stop...stop!"

When the torture is stopped, Tosca calls out to Mario to be sure. Mario assures her that they have stopped...and warns her not to speak. Again Scarpia asks her to tell him what she knows. Again she refuses. He calls to the executioner.

"No, no...monster...you're killing him!"

Her voice soars. Using the same melody, Scarpia tells her that it is her own silence that's doing it! He knows that he is going to win in the end. He laughs at her. She is even more tragic than on the stage! He orders more torture...as Tosca desperately tries not to tell him Angelotti's hiding place. But finally she can't stand it anymore and, with a dramatic high note, she begs him to end the agony...(as the music begins to play the melody of the flowing aria soon to come).

Once again she hears her lover's cry of pain. She calls to him—asking him to let her speak! But it's no use. Scarpia, full of rage, orders Spoletta to shut Mario up. Even Spoletta is shaken by these foul actions. When he comes back he starts to pray under his breath. And just at that moment Tosca can no longer resist. In a burst of sobbing she chokes out the words..."In the well...in the garden!" At this, Scarpia ends the torture. Spoletta tells him that the victim has fainted.

"Assassin! I want to see him!"

Cavaradossi is finally carried out covered with blood. Tosca is horrified! (The violins take up an unhappy strain.) She goes to kiss him...and slowly he comes to.

"Floria...!"

"Beloved..."

"Is that you?"

When he asks her if she said anything, she comforts him by saying she has kept his secret. Here's the chance Scarpia has been hoping for. In a loud voice, to be sure he's heard, he orders Spoletta to get Angelotti..."in the garden, in the well!"

As soon as Mario hears this, he tears himself away from Tosca cursing her for betraying him. She's torn with love for him, but he pushes her away.

Suddenly, Sciarrone rushes in with news that the Austrians have actually been *defeated* by Napoleon at the battle of Marenga! Bonaparte has won and General Melas has run.

This is all that Mario has to hear to get his strength back. In a glorious voice, reaching to the skies, he cries out, "Victory!...Victory!" Then, in a flood of joy, he quickly talks about how "the wicked tremble...liberty triumphs!" He turns to Scarpia and gloats that now "your heart trembles...you butcher!" But Scarpia shouts back at him that he will be taken away to be hanged! The policemen drag Mario out while Tosca tries to hold him back. But she's tossed aside and is left alone with the vile Scarpia.

She begs him to save Mario. Sarcastically Scarpia asks, "Who me ?" It's really up to her. He looks at his supper and smiling sadly comments at how it was "interrupted." Tosca is still at the door, crushed. He looks at her and suggests that she sit at the table and "let's see how we can save him." He offers her a bit of wine...wine from Spain. She ignores him as she steps forward. In an even voice she asks him, "How much?" She sits boldly, face to face.

"How much?" laughs Scarpia.

"What's the price?"

In a deep-toned aria, Scarpia again reveals how foul he is. Although he's interested in money, he doesn't sell himself to beautiful women. He wants a different kind of payment...if he's going to "betray his oath" as the chief of police. He's waited for just this moment. He had always been burning for her, but tonight when he saw her cry...it just made him want her more! The more he saw hate in her eyes, the more passion he felt for her! He rises to grasp her in his arms. Tosca leaps away and runs toward the window, threatening to jump. But Scarpia has

Mario...and so he has control over her.

Tosca is filled with contempt for the "vile devil"! He still tries to reach her as she flees from him in terror. For a moment she thinks of getting help from the Queen downstairs, but Scarpia reminds her that she would only be granting pardon to a dead man. Then, just as Tosca is desperately calling for help, there is the sound of drums in the distance. They are the drums that march the condemned to their death!

"Your Mario...hasn't more than an hour of life."

It's up to her. What will she do? The cold Scarpia stands waiting. From the very depth of her soul, Tosca now sings one of the most famous (and most sung) arias in opera. (The main melody was heard right in the beginning when she first went to the Church of Sant'Andrea della Valle and placed flowers at the statue of the Madonna.) It is sung softly and sweetly with deep passion, as Puccini directed, with one brilliant, dramatic high note near the very end.

> "I lived for art, I lived for love, not doing any harm to any living creature! Always with a sincere faith...I prayed in the holy chapels...always with a sincere faith, I gave flowers for the altar. In this hour of sorrow...why...why...Lord...why are you repaying me in this way?"

She has given jewels for the Madonna's gown...songs for the stars so that they might shine brighter. Then, repeating her question to the Lord...

> "Why, Lord, why are you repaying me in this way?"

She turns and again begs Scarpia for mercy. He will grant her wishes...but at a price that fills her with disgust. Just then, there's a knock on the door. It's Spoletta reporting that Angelotti has killed himself. Without turning a hair, Scarpia simply orders that they hang him dead on the gibbet. What about the other prisoner? Everything is ready for his execution. Tosca is sick at heart. Scarpia asks his spy to wait and turns to Tosca. The violins sound her misery.

"Well?"

Unable to see any other way out, Tosca nods her head as she covers her face and cries with shame.

She insists that Mario be freed at once, but Scarpia convinces her that his death must be faked. . .so that he, as chief of police, will not be blamed for freeing his prisoner. Spoletta will arrange everything. . .and she can hear the orders herself. To hurried, threatening music, Scarpia tells Spoletta that Cavaradossi will be shot (Tosca is startled)—but the way it was done with Count Palmieri: a *fake* execution. Do you understand? Spoletta really understands.

Tosca is not yet satisfied. She wants to explain the scheme to Mario herself. So Scarpia orders Spoletta to let her pass— and then at four o'clock. . ."like Palmieri."

The moment the spy is finally gone, Scarpia turns passionately to Tosca. She stops him. She wants a note of safe passage so that she and her lover can flee Rome forever! Why not? Scarpia goes to his desk. By which road? The shortest one. How about Civitavecchia? Fine.

However, there is one detail that Scarpia does not yet know about. When Tosca went to the dining table to help herself with a sip of wine, she saw a knife! And as she watches Scarpia every second, answering his questions as calmly as she can, her hands reach behind her looking for the knife. She finds it at last! (The violins play sweeping strains.) Not a moment too soon! Scarpia has put his seal to the note, and without wasting a minute he strides anxiously toward his prize.

"Tosca. . .finally mine!"

But his shout of passion is suddenly changed to a scream of pain! Tosca has stabbed him with a vengeance!

"This is the kiss of Tosca!" she cries in triumph.

The dying Scarpia calls weakly for help. He tries to rise from the floor by grabbing at the sofa...but he cannot. Tosca can't stop gloating over the evil Scarpia.

"Are you choking on blood?

And killed by a woman!

Did you torture me enough?

Do you still hear me? Speak!

Look at me! I am Tosca! Oh, Scarpia!"

He still tries to get help, but cannot, and at last falls back dead. Tosca is filled with anger at the man who wanted to ruin her. She wants him to die "damned"! She repeats over and over... "Die! Die! Die!" Then she sees that the figure on the floor is no longer moving. Scarpia is dead...and now, only now, will she forgive him! She looks down and moves away as she utters some of the most famous words in opera:

"And before him trembled all of Rome!"

Again the violins set the gloomy mood. Tosca can't stand the blood on her fingers. She goes to the table, wets a napkin with water and wipes the stains away. Where is the note? She searches the desk, but it can't be found! Then she sees it. It is grasped in Scarpia's fist! She shudders as she forces it from the dead fingers. Slowly she goes to the dinner table and blows out the candle. She turns to go, but something stops her. It is her inner sense of respect for the dead. She can't just leave him there.

But what can she do? She turns back, goes to the candle on the desk and with it, again lights the candle she had just blown out. Then, to the faint sound of her musical theme—and in time to two soft bass notes—she places first one candle then the other on each side of Scarpia's head. She looks around the room. She sees a crucifix hanging on the wall and with great care removes it, goes to the dead man once again and places it on his chest. She rises quickly (the drums begin to rumble), then slowly, carefully, goes out the door trailing her cape on the floor. And to the sound of the strings, the curtain falls.

ACT III

How was our composer going to follow an act so tremendously powerful, so full of deep human emotions, so terrible in action? He goes to the opposite end of the scale and has an innocent shepherd boy singing a lonesome tune at the beginning of the act.

Puccini was known to be one of those people who wanted everything to be as perfect as possible. So when he thought of having the boy sing, he had to have a song that was like those sung around the Roman hills. And instead of having his librettest write the words, he went to a poet, Luigi Zanazzo, who wrote the right words in the Roman dialect! Not only that, but when he decided to open the third act with church bells, he had to know the exact tone of the largest bell of St. Peter's! This time he went to his friend Father Pietro Panichelli who introduced him to a cathedral organist. But that wasn't enough for him. One morning Puccini climbed to the top of the fort—the Castel Sant'Angelo where the action takes place—and listened for himself! He put down every note of every bell and then directed which ones were to sound close, half-way, and far off!

When the curtain rises, it is not yet dawn. In the dim light the ramparts can be seen...with the great dome of St. Peter's in the distance. There is a fanfare of horns, and as the music lightens along with the sky, the clear sound of the shepherd boy's voice is heard. The delicate flutes accompany him. It's a sad little tune...very different from the violence that has just passed. Soon the church bells sound all over Rome calling the faithful to their morning prayers.

A jailer with a lantern arrives. In a moment, guards bring in Mario so the jailer can register his name. (The melody that Mario is soon to sing begins...with its longing, tragic and dramatic force.)

The prisoner has one last request. If the jailer will allow him to write a farewell note to "a dear person he will leave behind" he will give him his gold ring—the only thing of value that he has left. The jailer isn't quite sure, but then he agrees. So Mario tries to write to Floria but soon has to stop—overcome by his memories. The music picks up the melody of their duet in church. Then the oboe starts the wistful aria that Mario is about to sing. He remembers a happier time.

"The stars were shining...the earth was perfumed...the garden gate squeaked...and a footstep scattered the sand...she entered, fragrant...she fell into my arms..."

He remembers the sweet kisses, the soft caresses...her beautiful form. It has disappeared forever, his dream of love. The last hour of his life is also fleeing...and he is to die in desperation. Then, with a wonderful high note, his voice lingering on the word "love," he bitterly cries, "and I have never before loved life so much!" He tragically holds his head in his hands, as he can no longer hold back the tears.

Spoletta arrives with Tosca. He shows her where Mario is and she rushes to him, gently lifting up his head. The cymbals crash.

Mario can't believe his eyes! She shows him the note and they both read where they are to be set free! It's signed by Scarpia!

"His first favor is this one..."

"And his last!" declares Tosca.

She describes the vile bargain that Scarpia had proposed. In a strong, steady voice she tells him how she pleaded with that "monster" but he only laughed. She consented...even as she picked up the knife. Then as soon as he had written the pass and came after her...she stuck the blade into his heart.

Cavaradossi can't believe that those hands actually killed for love of him. He gently takes hold of them...and with lyrical softness he sings...

"Oh sweet hands so soft and pure...
hands meant for petting children, gathering roses...
to pray...for unfortunate ones....
Oh sweet hands so soft and pure...."

But Tosca wants him to know what he must do. She has already packed her gold and jewels, and a carriage is ready. First—and he'll laugh at this—he is to be "shot." At the shots, he must fall! When the soldiers leave and they are safe, they'll both flee to Civitavecchia where a ship will be waiting to carry them away!

"Free!"

"By way of the sea!"

Then with music that reminds us a little of *Butterfly*, Tosca asks,

"Who feels pain...anymore? Do you smell the scent of roses?"

She's filled with happiness. Mario can't say enough about how wonderful she is and how she is everything to him. His voice reaches upward. She, in turn, tells him that she will be his guiding love on earth...till the day comes when they will rise to the heavens...as light clouds above the sea. They are both in a dream-world.

But now to the "act." He is to fall at once, being careful not to hurt himself. Mario stops her and draws her close. He wants to hear again the love words that she has just spoken—the sound of her voice is so sweet. Both sing of their victory.

"With new hope...the soul trembles...the soul rises in an ecstacy of love!"

While the lovers have been in each others arms, the firing squad has taken its position. The "fake" execution is about to take place. Mario is bravely ready. Tosca again reminds him to go down at the first shot. They both can hardly keep from laughing.

The orchestra begins a mournful, driving sound. The horns

and drums are heard. Floria is impatient to get away. There!
They are finally taking aim! How handsome is her Mario. The
squad fires! Tosca is thrilled at the way her Mario has
"died"...he has fallen just like an actor! Now she warns him
not to move. The soldiers must all be gone. The steps fade as
does the music. Silence.

"Mario, up, quick! Let's go! Let's go! Up! Mario! Mario!"

She's stunned to discover he's really dead! Her terror turns
to cries of despair.

"Is this the way it ends? Like this?"

Suddenly voices and steps are heard. Spoletta and Sciarrone
rush in.

"There she is!"

"Ah, Tosca!" shouts Spoletta, trying to grab her. "You'll
dearly pay for his (Scarpia's) life!"

But Tosca, jumping to her feet, pushes him away. She tells
him that she *will* pay—with her own life—as she leaps to the
edge of the fort. Then, with a final cry, saying that both she and
Scarpia will meet before God...she falls to her death below!

The cymbals crash again...the orchestra repeats a familiar
melody...finally ending with a sudden short chord—the same
one that greeted Scarpia's entrance in the very first act! The
tragic scene ends with the body of Mario where it fell...while
the soldiers and two of Scarpia's men stand in shocked silence.

THE CURTAIN FALLS

With *Tosca*, Puccini showed that he could write music full of
tension and suspense...and not just music for delicate heroines
that brings tears to our eyes. The ending itself is packed with
such great force that we're left with a feeling of having run a race.

The legendary Sarah Bernhardt not only created a sensation

with her *Tosca*, but left many bits of stage action that have been used in the opera to the present day. One especially dramatic "business" is when she is leaving the dead Scarpia and the last thing seen is her cape slowly disappearing through the door.

It was surprising that the composer and the playwright had no real differences except for the ending. Sardau wanted Tosca to jump off the wall and into the Tiber River. The only problem with that is that she would have had to grow wings since the river is at least fifty feet away—and on the opposite side of the castle!

Again, Puccini had problems with his librettists, Illica and Giacosa. This work was so different from the lyrical tenderness of *Boheme* that they wondered if it could be any kind of an opera at all. But Puccini was convinced that *Tosca* would be a success. He hadn't figured on what happened opening night...

It is Sunday, January 14, 1900. Although the opera is set one hundred years earlier, the Rome of 1900 is still torn with revolution and riots. To make things worse, there is talk of a bunch of jealous rivals plotting against the composer and his new opera. On top of that, the Roman police have come in and warned the conductor, Leopoldo Mugnone (who was already scared to death), that a bomb might go off in the house.

In spite of all this, the music begins, but the audience is still whispering. Then they're talking and Mugnone is shaking. Finally, the noise gets so bad that the poor conductor stops the music, leaves his baton, and runs for his dressing room! What is the trouble? Well, instead of a plot, the arguing is about people coming in late and bothering those who are already in their seats. (Nothing has really changed.)

Anyway, the conductor is lured back and the opera is performed. Much to Puccini's disappointment, it is not greeted with great joy...or even mild enthusiasm. The story is so harsh that the critics and the audience can't take it. It is not another *Manon* or *Boheme*, full of poetry and lyrical music. (Even the opening at La Scala, Milan, on March 17 conducted by Toscanini, didn't make it!)

Yet its time was to come—and soon. In fact on July 12, in London's Covent Garden, *Tosca* was to receive the kind of excitement and raves that it has enjoyed ever since. The singers were outstanding: Fernando de Lucia as Mario, Milka Ternina as Tosca, and Antonio Scotti as Scarpia—one of the greatest who ever lived. Puccini was called to the stage by Conductor Mancinelli. Waves and waves of applause poured over them. *Tosca* had indeed arrived with a vengeance!

And at its American premiere at the Metropolitan, February 4, 1901, *Tosca* again triumphed and has been performed, year after year, almost as many times as the everlasting *La Boheme*.

Puccini went on to write *The Girl of the Golden West* (a western, again by David Belasco based on a story by Bret Harte). Other works followed. But *Turandot*, his last, and some think his best, was left unfinished.

At the age of sixty-six, doctors discovered throat cancer! Hurriedly, the Puccinis traveled to Brussels for the dangerous operation. For awhile it seemed that the master would live. But before too long a heart attack struck. He died in Brussels on November 29, 1924. In Rome the news shocked the city and especially those who were, even then, listening to his *Boheme*. The opera stopped and the standing audience listened in tears to the Funeral March by Frederick Chopin.

Today, Puccini—along with his wife and son—rests in a crypt in the walls of the tiny chapel of the villa he loved so much at Torre del Lago. To visit it is to go back to the days when he sat at his piano all night long composing music about the human heart, music for which the whole world will be forever grateful.

Once again we put on our traveling shoes and wait to see where the world of opera will take us next. As we get ready to leave Rome, we'll take with us the memories of the Church of Sant'Andrea, the Farnese Palace, and the Castle of Sant'Angelo with its huge statue of St. Michael flying at the very top. Built on the tomb of the Emperor Hadrian, this fort has been the refuge of the Pope in times of danger. In fact, it is said that it is actually connected to the Vatican (where the Pope lives) by way of a secret passage.

We see the ruins of the Roman Forum, once the heart of the empire, with its white marble columns and other signs of past glory. There's the giant frosty memorial to King Victor Emanuel—that looks like a big "wedding cake" to many Italians. And on the edge of a large square is the skeleton of the amazing Coliseum where chariots raced and gladiators died.

We remember, too, the magnificent Fontana di Trevi, the Trevi Fountain. . .with its herioc statues and rearing horses. . .where we tossed a coin over our shoulder so that our wish to return would be granted. . .to see once more all the flowers covering the Spanish Steps. . .where the great English poets Byron, Keats and Shelley loved to roam. And to admire—at every turn—the over two thousand fountains that splash and murmur throughout the ancient city.

But now, why not go from the tragic world of *Tosca* to a place far different. . .resting partly in France and partly in Spain. It is called the Basque region, close to the lofty Pyrenees that loom high into the sky. We'll be visiting a lot of country folk who are full of fun—and easily fooled.

The story for this next opera was taken from a French comedy—*Le Philtre*—by August-Eugene Scribe, and was made into a delightful comic opera by another master composer. . .Gaetano Donizetti (Gie-TAH-no Dun-ee-ZET-ti).

The Elixir of Love—the love potion—has been giving audiences heart-felt chuckles ever since it was presented in the Teatro della Canobbiana in Milan, Italy, on May 12, 1832. It is hard to imagine that a work with so much melody, that has been bringing joy to so many for over one hundred and fifty years, was composed in only two weeks! But then there were a good many musical geniuses in those days.

When Donizetti heard that his fellow composer Rossini (who was his hero) had taken only a month to write *The Barber of Seville*, he thought a moment then said, . . . "he's so lazy." (Actually Rossini wrote it in about two weeks.)

Luckily, he had a librettist (who used to be a lawyer), Felice Romani, who proved he could write beautiful poetry by doing Bellini's *Norma*. He also proved he could write as fast as Donizetti wanted him to.

The composer asked him to do the opera in the spring of 1832. "I've got. . .fourteen days. I give you a week to do your part." He then added that despite having a German soprano, a stuttering tenor, a baritone with the "voice of a goat" and a bass who isn't very much—"we must cover ourselves with glory." And so they did, as we shall soon see!

One wonders if Donizetti's sense of humor was born in him. Certainly he didn't think it was very funny when his father wanted him to be an architect! By the age of nine—having spent time mostly daydreaming and writing pieces of music—his father gave up and put him into the Lezioni Caritatevoli di Musica in Bergamo. . .the little town where he was born.

By ten he was tops in the school. His teacher Giovanni Simone Mayr, continued to teach his star pupil singing, harpsichord and musical forms until he was seventeen. (In between—at eleven—the boy sang in student operas composed by his teacher. At first he was a mezzo soprano but finally, six years later, he sang as a bass! All along he was noted for his ready good humor and comic behavior. Certainly his study of voice helped him greatly in composing operas that have been so "singable.")

Then Mayr thought he should go to the Liceo Filarmonica Comunale in Bologna.

At eighteen Donizetti wrote *Il Pigmalione*—his first opera—in seven days! The next year he came back to his home town, and by January 28, 1822, at the ripe old age of twenty-four, his fourth opera, *Zoraide di Granata*, was a huge success at the opera house in Rome.

And so it went. . . writing, writing, writing. . . all kinds of music from string quartets to solemn masses, and of course operas—sixty-seven in all!

But now it's time to meet some new friends near a small village in the mountainous Basque country. It is the 1800's. The golden curtain is about to go up on. . .

2

L'Elisir D'Amore

(Leh-lee-ZEER Da-MOH-reh)

ACT I

On her rich farm the young, attractive Adina (ah-DEEN-ah) is about to entertain her best friend Giannetta (Gee-a-NET-tah) and some farm-hands with a story. They're all under a spreading tree to keep out of the noon-day sun. We hear a fanfare in the prelude (the beginning) and flutes that set the light, cheery scene. Then a pretty melody is played that will soon be sung by all. They sing about how comfortable they are out of the "boiling" sun resting in the shade on the side of a hill. They're keeping cool...amidst fragrant flowers...alongside the flowing river.

BUT...from the flaming passion of love, neither shade nor river can protect them! Lucky is the worker who can guard himself against it!

Meanwhile, off to one side, too shy and too much in love to join them, stands Nemorino (Neh-more-EEN-oh). He's gazing at his true love, Adina, and is overcome by her loveliness. He sings a slightly bouncy, yet flowing, aria...a form of music known as a *cavatina*.

"How beautiful she is...how dear she is! The more I see her, the more I love her..."

But he feels that she's so much better than he... "she reads, studies..." while he will always be "an idiot..." who can do nothing more than "sigh."

"Who will open up my mind? Who will teach me how to be loved?"

Sure enough, the love-sick Nemorino is completely ignored. Instead, Adina begins to laugh at the story she's been reading. She thinks it's ridiculous! The group wants to know what is making her so amused. They want her to share it with them. Adina explains that it is the legend about Tristan (an English knight)...a tale of love. They beg her to read it...read it! (We hear Nemorino deciding to get closer without being seen.)

So in a sweet waltz, Adina tells them about the "cruel Isolde" (an Irish princess) who wants nothing to do with Tristan (TRIS-tahn). But then, on his knees, he begs a wise magician for help. And so he receives a small bottle of an "elixir of love"...which will make the beautiful Isolde "no longer able to run from him!" She goes on...and the chorus joins in.

"Elixir so perfect...of such rare quality..."

No one knows what it is made of...or how it is made. Adina keeps on reading. As soon as Tristan took a sip from the magic bottle, Isolde (E-ZOLE-deh) instantly had a change of heart. The "beautiful but cruel one" fell in love with Tristan and became his forevermore! Adina hits a long, high note. All sing together again.

Just as they end, there's the sound of military drums and cheerful marching music. What is it? Who can it be? Well, into the

scene strides the bragging, swinging Belcore (Bell-COH-reh)—
sergeant of the village guard. He's a sight to see in his blazing
uniform and gold braid.

*(Belcore—which means "good heart"—like all the characters
in the show—is really a pleasant fellow. He thinks a lot of
himself, but with good humor. He never really hurts
anyone. . .or is hurt himself. Donizetti created a work in which
there is no meanness in any of his main characters. In this
sense it is not like "The Barber of Seville"—an opera buffa—
where Dr. Bartolo really had a hard time. . .but an opera
comica where everybody is full of fun.)*

Belcore quickly, and with chest out, goes to Adina and com-
paring himself to the "gallant Paris" (the Trojan prince who gave
an apple to Aphrodite, the goddess of love), gives her a bou-
quet of flowers.

"My delicious little vixen. . .I bring you these flowers."

But he is more "glorious" than Paris. . .happier than him
because as a prize for his gift, he will steal away her heart!

At this Adina comments that this young man is quite modest.

"Yes, that's true," sings the chorus.

While Nemorino is in "despair," Belcore goes on to brag that
he is not surprised to see that he has won Adina's heart.

"I am gallant, I'm a sergeant. . .No beauty can resist. . ."

Then in a flowery way he sings that even the goddess of love
was conquered by Mars, the god of war!

Once again Adina notes how "modest" he is, to which the
others agree, "Yes, truly." When Nemorino hears his beloved
laughing, he's sadder than ever at the thought that she is laughing
with Belcore and against *him*.

The sergeant, full of confidence, suggests that since Adina
loves him as he loves her. . .why not get married? But Adina
is not in a hurry. She wants a little time to think about it.
(Nemorino is beside himself: if she should accept, he will simply
die!)

With a nice melody, Belcore reminds Adina that time flies by..."the days and the hours"...so give in to the winner..."from me you can't escape!" Adina soon joins him, singing that these men quickly think they are winners before they have even begun to fight! She's not so easily caught! Now Nemorino gets into the act. All three hurry along and get louder and louder. He wishes that love would give him the kind of courage he needs. Instead, he is "too timid" and cannot say what he feels.

Into all this Gianetta and the chorus remark that it surely would be laughable if Adina does get caught by that soldier. Adina hits a big, high note.

> "Yes, yes," sings the crowd, "but she (Adina) is an old smarty...and will not be captured."

So Belcore, changing the subject, asks if he and his soldiers can rest awhile under the shady trees. Of course! In fact, Adina is happy to even offer them a bottle of wine. Belcore is sure that he's already "a member of the family"!

By now the sun is going down, so Adina tells her peasants to quit work for the day. They all slowly go out with the sergeant and Giannetta, leaving Nemorino and Adina alone.

> "Just one word," begins the shy Nemorino.

Adina is annoyed at the same old thing, the same old sighs. (She would really like him to be more forceful since she truly loves him.)

> "You would do better if you went to the city to visit your uncle who is so very sick."

> "His sickness is nothing compared to mine! I've tried a thousand times to leave—but I can't.

Suppose his uncle dies and leaves his money to somebody else? He doesn't care. Adina points out that he would then die of hunger!

> "Whether I die of hunger or of love...to me it's all the same!"

She tries to talk some sense into him (and to get him to be more aggressive). She calls him a "good boy"...modest...not like that bragging sergeant. But she's very fickle and changeable, so it's useless for him to hope for her love.

"Oh, Adina...why not ever?"

"A fine question that is!"

In a very pretty duet, Adina explains that trying to get her is like catching a breeze that "flies without resting...going from a lily over to a rose..." That's just the kind of girl she is. It's her "nature." Nemorino wants to know what he should do then.

"Forget about my loving you...just go away."

"Dear Adina...I can't!"

"You can't? Why not?"

Nemorino repeats her question..."Why? Why?" He'll tell her why. With the same lyrical melody, he tells her to ask a steady river why it runs down to the sea where it "dies" away. Adina continues to prod him along. So? He will die like the river...die following her. Then he should find another! But this would be impossible for him...impossible, impossible! And so Adina plays hard to get while Nemorino will not give in...their voices blending in a slow melody, finally reaching a brilliant high note as they gradually leave the scene.

As with Tristan and Isolde, they are really in love—without needing a love potion—but Adina just hasn't admitted it to herself. Yet love always finds a way, as we shall see.

When the curtain goes up again, we are in the main plaza of the village. The people are busily coming and going. Suddenly, the fanfare of a cornet (a brass wind instrument like a trumpet) is heard! What can it be? Who is it? What is it? They all strain to see. (The horn is the signal for the quack doctor—Dulcamara—to arrive. The original directions call for him to travel in a splendid carriage. But some productions have him drop in from a large colorful balloon, slowly drifting down in the middle of the square. Which ever way he shows up, he's a sight to see in his gorgeous clothes.) All the peasants are overwhelmed. They have never seen such a "grand person." He must be a baron...a marquis...perhaps a duke...or even more!

Here's the perfect con man...a flim-flam man of the highest order. Without wasting a minute, "Doctor" Dulcamara (Dool-cah-MAH-rah)...a name which means "bittersweet," starts right in giving his sales talk.

> "Listen! Listen...Oh, country-folk...Attention...I am that great physician...an encyclopedic doctor named Dulcamara...known all over the world...and other places!"

He's got a medicine that cures everything. Buy it! His magic medicine made a seventy year old man young again..."grand-father to ten babies!" It's great for making skin soft. It makes young men terrific lovers. Buy this wonderful potion...he'll sell it for very little. It makes the paralyzed walk again! It cures apoplexy, asthma, deafness, diabetes, liver ailments (and anything else).

> "How much does it cost? How much is a bottle worth? A hundred? Thirty? Twenty? NO! To prove my good inten-tions...to all my friends gathered here...I give it to you...my good people... for only one ordinary dollar!" (approximately)

The crowd is amazed at the promises of this rapid-fire pitch...and especially by the low cost!

> "One dollar! Truly, a finer man we've never known..."

Now Dulcamara has a special bargain. His "stupendous" potion—all Europe knows—he sells for no less than nine *lire*. But because he actually was born in this part of the country...he will let them have it for three! (All this to a happy cornet sound.)

Well, everyone thinks he's the greatest thing that ever hap-pened to them. And with a lilting chorus, they end by saying that "his arrival they will long remember!" They surely will.

It seems to Nemorino that this "miracle man" was sent to him from heaven! He wants to know more about this wonderful science. He goes to Dulcamara and asks him a very important question.

"Do you have, by any chance, the love potion of Queen Isolde?"

This hits the fake doctor like a pie in the face. He not only doesn't know anything about a love potion...he's never even heard of Isolde.

"Huh? What? What's that?"

But it doesn't take him long to get a hold of the situation. (They are about to begin a bubbling duet.) Oh...*that* love potion. Well, he's the very one who *makes* it! And it's in great demand. Nemorino is overjoyed...especially when he is told that he can really buy some. After all, Dulcamara sells it every day to the whole world.

Now comes the question of how much it costs. The young man has very little money. He doesn't know that it doesn't matter. Sure enough, when he mentions that he only has a few cents, Dulcamara tells him that it is exactly the price of the potion! So Nemorino quickly turns over his money as the doctor grandly hands over the bottle.

They both sing a lively, cheerful tune. On his part, Nemorino can't thank Dulcamara enough. He's so happy, so contented...at such generosity. The Doctor, on the other hand, has never met a dummy to equal the one he's just found!

"Hey, Doctor—just a second—how do I take it?"

All he has to do is shake it a bit, open it carefully so that the "vapor" doesn't get away, put it to his mouth and take a good swig. It won't be long before he'll feel the full effect. No, not at once—it'll take a whole day. (Just enough time for the good doctor to get away!)

"What about the taste?"

"It's excellent!" (After all, it's Bordeaux wine, not potion.)

And so Nemorino starts all over again thanking Dulcamara. He's so "obligated" to this "blessed" doctor for this great elixir.

In a fast little duet—another marvelous melody—Dulcamara warns him not to tell anyone about it. If they all find out he has love for sale, he may easily end up in jail.

Nemorino promises not to tell a soul. He has no intention of sharing even a drop with anybody else...since he wants the potion to turn Adina around...he'll drink the whole bottle himself. With that, Dulcamara takes off.

Nemorino can hardly stand it. He hugs the wonderful bottle. It's all for him! Even *before* he drinks it he's already feeling great! He takes a big sip. Then another. Now he really begins to feel good. How come he has to wait for tomorrow? This stuff is delicious...and he already is getting light-headed as well as light-hearted. He sits down, takes out something to eat and joyfully sings some aimless la-la-ra-ras!

Who should walk in on this tipsy scene? None other than Adina! Who the dickens is that fool? Is she dreaming or is that really Nemorino? And why is he so cheerful?

As soon as he spots Adina, Nemorino gets up to rush to her—but suddenly stops in his tracks. Why should he bore her with his sighs? All he has to do is wait for tomorrow, and her cold heart will "adore" him!

"Lara, lara, la, lara...," sings Nemorino.

"I don't know whether he's faking or really happy..."

From the corner of his eye, Nemorino is wondering if she has yet begun to love him. Reaching a soaring note, Adina decides that his lack of interest in her must be put on. She laughs at the thought.

Here we have another beautiful duet. Nemorino singing that she had better get all laughing in now...for tomorrow will be another story...while Adina is sure of the hold she has on him—

the "chains of love"—which no amount of fake indifference can break!

"Yes, yes, yes...tomorrow she will love me," softly ends Nemorino's song.

He starts his tipsy singing all over again. Well, this is too much for Adina. She's really wondering what's come over him. (Is she getting some pangs of jealousy?) She goes to him.

"Good for you! I see you've learned your lesson!"

"That's for sure! I'm trying it out to see how it works!"

"Then all your love-pains...?"

"Are forgotten I hope..."

"What about the old flame?"

"It's dying out a little at a time...by tomorrow it should be gone!"

And with this, he starts his little song once more—that she had better laugh while she can, for by tomorrow "she will love him."

To herself, Adina again thinks that although the dummy is trying to "break his chains"...by tomorrow he'll find them heavier than ever!

Before they can go on, there's Belcore's voice. He comes in with some others. He has shown up just in time! She's going to use the sergeant to make Nemorino think twice. She starts out by giving Belcore the idea that perhaps the "fortress" (her heart) can be conquered after all. He can hardly believe his ears! Is it possible? (Meanwhile, Nemorino is shaking, in spite of himself.)

"When are we going to get married?" sings Belcore, not wasting any time.

"Very soon."

"But *when*?"

"In six days..."

"Oh, joy...I'm so happy!"

Nemorino, now sure of the power of the potion, laughs out loud. They begin a merry trio mixed in with a lovely flowing strain. Belcore wonders what that "silly idiot" is laughing at. If he doesn't go away, he'll punch him in the head! Adina is furious at the thought that her former slave is so cheery even when he knows she's going to get married to someone else.

"I can no longer hide how angry he is making me!"

Nemorino, of course, isn't worried about Belcore since tomorrow will change everything.

Before anything else can happen, some drums are heard. Soldiers, Giannetta and the peasants come in. She tells Belcore that his men have been looking everywhere for him. Well, he's here...what's the trouble? The soldier's chorus explain that they have an order that was left for him. The guard has been transferred to other quarters! The soldiers are shocked and disappointed to find that they have to leave the next morning. They're always being moved around and are always leaving their girlfriends!

"My dearest, did you hear? Tomorrow is goodbye! At least, remember my love for you..."

Nemorino now can't wait for tomorrow. But before he can jump for joy, Belcore gets an idea. If in six days—why wait? Why not right away? How about today? Adina looks over at Nemorino. He's got his mouth open in horror. Good! That's just what she wants to see.

"All right...today"

"Today! Oh, Adina...did you say *today*?"

"And why not?" demands Adina, hands on hips.

"At least wait till tomorrow!" pleads Nemorino.

In a sad refrain, the unhappy young man begs her to wait. "Adina believe me...wait awhile..." Belcore can't stand it. If it wasn't that the "donkey" was full of wine, he'd haul off and give him a good clout on the head.

"Go away, you clown, get away from me..."

Adina tries to excuse Nemorino by calling him "just a boy...a misfit who is half crazy...who has it in his head that she must love *him* just because he's delirious with love for *her!*" (She thinks of how sweet her revenge is. She wants him to feel sorry and fall at her feet.)

Everybody joins in a sad chorus. Giannetta can't imagine *where* that "simpleton" got that idea...everyone can see that the sergeant is a man of the world, without equal—a man just right for the beautiful Adina.

Nemorino is frantic! All his plans for tomorrow are going down the drain. He desperately calls for the "doctor" to help him...help! Adina is smug. Belcore calls for a dance and a banquet. All look forward to a great time..."dancing and feasting" as the violins set up a catchy tune.

The feverish Nemorino, seeing the sergeant smiling at him...Adina ungrateful...the crowd laughing in rhythm...calls for the Doctor to help him—to have pity on him—as the drums roll and the curtain falls. (It must be said again that all of this seemingly unhappy-for-Nemorino scene is done with great good humor, playful, but not cruel...just "bittersweet"!)

ACT II

Trumpets sound as the curtain rises on a happy scene. Adina, Belcore, Dulcamara and Giannetta are sitting around the festive table, while the country folk are dancing and singing. It's another pleasant, bouncy tune that comes to a swirling end.

"Let's sing, let's make toasts to the so-much-in-love bride and groom. For them may the days be long and peaceful..."

As for Belcore, he thinks that the best of all possible worlds is when he has "love and wine...a woman and a glass."

But Adina is wondering whatever happened to Nemorino. She

would like to see him here. The chorus goes on its merry way repeating their joyful song. At the first chance, Dulcamara gets up and bids everybody to listen to him. He has a little song... a brand new one...lively and graceful...which he will sing if the beautiful bride will join him. Everyone is anxious to have the "grand" Dulcamara perform. It must be a "rare thing"—this song—if *he* wants to do it!

So from his pocket the Doctor takes out the song in two parts—one for Adina and one for him. It's titled "Nina, the Lady Gondolier and Senator Tredenti." To the light accompaniment of violins, this pretty *barcarole* begins.

"I am rich and you are lovely...I've got money and you have charm... And since for me you are my beauty, dear Nina, what more do you want?" clowns Senator Tredenti (Three Teeth).

Adina plays right along.

"What an honor! A senator! Wants me to love him."

Adina, playing hard to get, goes on to tell him that "someone else wants to marry me." Well, let's not have any more argument—make a senator happy. But "Nina," insists Adina, "is not worthy of a senator!" The delightful playing back and forth goes on until she sings that a young man—Zanetto—likes her and wants to marry her.

The chorus joins in and congratulates Dulcamara on a truly "rare" song expertly sung! To which he modestly admits that Doctor Dulcamara is a "professor" of every art!

In walks the lawyer who will set up the marriage vows.

"Quiet!" commands Belcore. "Here's the notary who has come to complete my happiness."

They all greet this important man. Dulcamara, of course, goes overboard by declaring that he "embraces and salutes...this doctor of love!" Adina is more than annoyed; she's worried. The lawyer has arrived and Nemorino hasn't! Belcore notices the pain in her eyes. She brushes off his question. (If Nemorino isn't present, how can her vengeance be complete?) She's trying to convince herself that that is all it is, but we know better. So with Belcore hurrying the unwilling Adina along, and the chorus again singing about a toast, the entire company leaves the stage.

All except Dulcamara. A wedding ceremony is nice enough, but he's not going anywhere while all the goodies are on the banquet table! At last Nemorino shows up. He's really down. He saw the notary...all hope is gone...his heart is breaking. The Doctor is still at the table singing his song under his breath.

"You're here, Doctor!

Yes, he was invited to dinner by the newlyweds and so he's passing the time by eating. Nemorino is desolate. He had hoped that he would be loved before tomorrow, but it hasn't happened. Dulcamara thinks he's batty. What he needs is another "dose" of the potion. (Only the piano accompanies this conversation.)

"Will she really love me?"

Of course! Dulcamara assures him that *everybody* will love him. Some more elixir will do the job. (He'll be gone in half an hour anyway.) Does the young man have any money for another bottle? Alas, Nemorino hasn't got a cent left. Oh, in that case, the whole picture is changed. But as soon as he has some, he should come to find Dulcamara. He still has about a quarter of an hour. And with that, the Doctor leaves.

Nemorino flings himself onto a seat. How unlucky he is. Into this sad scene walks Belcore. He'll never be able to understand women! Here Adina says she loves him and will marry him...but she wants to postpone the ceremony till tonight!

Nemorino looks at his rival. How he would love to crack his head with his fist. Belcore spots him.

"Hey, hey...young man...what's making you so desperate?"

"...I haven't any money and I don't know where to find some."

"Hey, dummy! If you haven't any money, become a soldier and you'll get twenty dollars!"

This is a big surprise to Nemorino. Twenty dollars! And he'll get it right away. What to do? Belcore, in a flowery way, describes how great it will be in the regiment. And if it's love he wants, well, he'll have plenty. A duet begins. Nemorino soulfully sings of the dangers of war...of leaving his uncle and his friends. But what else can he do? If he can have even one day with Adina...he'll be ready to "lose his life!" Yes, he'll be ready to lose his life.

The sergeant, in a speedy sales pitch, talks of the wonderful roll of the drums and flags flying, not to mention all the girls.

Finally, thinking again of the money he'll get, Nemorino decides to join. Good, he has only to sign the papers. As soon as Nemorino makes his mark, Belcore is very happy. In one stroke he has at last gotten rid of his competition. He laughs at how clever he is.

With sweeping sadness Nemorino reflects that Belcore doesn't really know why he has joined the army. He doesn't realize the kind of heart that beats under Nemorino's common clothes. He doesn't know how much money means. No "treasure" can equal it—if it helps him gain Adina's love! His voice soars, the violins play...as the scene ends.

At the next curtain, we see Giannetta and all her girlfriends. They're stunned at some news. As the violins plink along, they are wondering.

"Can it be possible?" whisper the girls.

"Extremely possible," says Giannetta.

"It isn't probable?"

"Very probable!"

"But how come? How do you know? Who told you?"

"Not so loud!"

As soon as they hear that it was the owner of the fabric store who told Giannetta—in the strictest confidence—they all believe the story. And what is that? Nemorino's uncle has died and left him his entire fortune! He's a millionaire! Lucky is the girl who marries him! But for now it's a secret. They must not mention a thing. Not a thing!

Just at this moment they spot the lucky man walking along. They all bunch to one side as they look at the new rich one. Nemorino hasn't yet heard the good news.

He's been drinking out of his great big bottle of "love potion". . . and it has already made him tipsy. He sings about how much he has been drinking of "this marvelous elixir." Now he'll have all the girls chasing him (the Doctor promised). He has high hopes. In fact, he's already beginning to see results. He must go.

But the girls stop him. They see that he doesn't yet know about his good luck.

"Your humble servant!" starts Giannetta.

One after the other, the girls greet him with curtsies. Nemorino can't figure out what has come over these "youngsters."

"That Nemorino is a real dear. . .," sing the girls. "He has the look of a lord," they repeat.

Oh, now he knows! *It's the elixir that's finally begun to work!* He understands! He understands! It's the magic potion!

In walk Adina and Dulcamara. She's startled. The boy she really loves is surrounded by girls. (Nemorino may be a farm boy, but he's not as dumb as they think!)

"What do I see?"

"Oh, poor boy!" declares Dulcamara. "To show how much they care, they're tearing him to pieces!"

Nemorino is ecstatic. He tells the Doctor how much he owes that rare elixir. They all love him! Adina can't believe her ears.

All the girls want him to go with them to the dance. Adina wants to talk to him. What about?

"Later...later," sing the girls, "let's go to the dance..."

"Sure, to the dance," agrees the delighted Nemorino, "but don't kill me!"

And off they drag him.

Adina, of course, doesn't care for this one bit...as she comments how happily Nemorino went along. Doctor Dulcamara can't resist his chance. He admits that it really is all his fault. How come? He can create joy at will...with his wonderful recipes! Adina thinks that's crazy.

"Crazy, you say?...Do you know the great power of the love potion used by Queen Isolde?"

Again, Adina can't believe what she's hearing. He gave Nemorino that potion? Sure, so that he could get the love of "a cruel one." Adina now knows how much Nemorino loves her. So much that he gave up his "liberty" for her—he became a soldier so he could buy more of the Elixir of Love! The orchestra hits a chord. A gentle duet is about to begin.

"How much love! And I, spiteful one, tormented that noble heart!"

Even Dulcamara is now convinced that his potion really works. Adina herself has become a victim of it! (The beautiful melody we hear is very similar to the music Donizetti wrote later in his tragic *Lucia Di Lammermoor*.) Adina reflects that finally Nemorino is lucky in love. Dulcamara doesn't help things very much by agreeing that all the young women have gone crazy over him. She wonders which one of all the girls Nemorino has chosen. Again, the Doctor gives the wrong answer by saying that *everyone* follows him...all want him. Adina recalls that she alone, "the dumbbell," had full "possession of that noble heart." She can't help crying at the thought...as she repeats it again to herself. However, Dulcamara has a solution. What can it be? Well, if she would like, he will make up a recipe for *her* which will make her irresistible. The tune is spritely as Adina's voice becomes colorful and flowery, flitting from note to note.

"Ah! Doctor...your potions are great...but they would not work for me."

"Would you like to see a million lovers sighing and falling at your feet?"

"I wouldn't know what to do with so many; my heart longs for only one."

No amount of promises from the Doctor will convince Adina to take his potion. She has "respect" for his elixir, but it's not for her.

"...I have a better one: Nemorino will leave all the others to be only for me, mine alone."

The Doctor, at last, realizes that she is much too wise—even wiser than he! (Remember Rosina?)

In a lovely, lyrical melody, Adina explains the power she has within her.

"A little tender glance...a smile...a caress...and from me (high note) Nemorino cannot flee..."

Dulcamara sees that she is smarter than his magic. Her beautiful mouth specializes in the art of love...and she can get any "lover she wants." In fact, he wouldn't mind exchanging his bottles of elixir for the kind of power that she possesses! And with that, Adina and the Doctor leave.

The scene is deserted. Slowly the figure of Nemorino appears. The stage is set for the most famous aria of the opera. To the gentle strains of the harp and the smooth sound of the wooden bassoon, Nemorino gives us a final view of how much he loves Adina. (Donizetti, over-ruling his librettist's strong objections, actually stops the show by putting an emotion-packed song right in the way of the fast-moving comical action. Of course, he was right—as every performance of this melodious opera proves.) Nemorino sings of what he saw...a secret tear in her eyes.

"One furtive tear...her eyes spilled over...what more do I want? She loves me, yes, she loves me...I saw it! For one single moment I heard the beat of her heart! I heard the throbbing...my sighs mixed in with hers! Heavens!...one could die of love...I ask for no more... one could die of love..."

The last words "of love" are held in one long breath...bringing the aria to a graceful, moving end.

He sees Adina coming toward him. He believes she's even more gorgeous than ever because of her "growing love." Adina goes right up to him and demands to know what's going on. He doesn't know where he stands anymore...both young girls and old ones, pretty and ugly...all want him for a husband! He doesn't know what to do. All right, listen. Nemorino is all ears since he surely expects to hear words of love from Adina.

"Why did you decide to become a soldier?"

"...because I wanted to see if I could improve myself," fibs Nemorino.

Adina ignores that and comes right to the point. His life is precious to her, so she has bought back the contract from Belcore!

Nemorino is overcome that she, herself, has done this! (Of course...it's the potion working!) Adina begins her own melodious *cavatina*. She offers him the paper.

"Take it, take it...through me you're free; stay here on your native soil...here where everyone loves you..."

To the plinking of violins, Adina, through a whole variety of wonderful vocal gymnastics, tells him that he will be unhappy if he leaves...so he should stay. She climbs to a glorious high note as the aria comes to a close. Nemorino has listened in rapture to his beloved's *fioritura* (flowery singing), and now expects her to declare her love. Instead...

"Goodbye!"

"*What*? You're leaving me."

"Yes—me."

"Don't you have something else to tell me?"

"Nothing else."

Well, this starts him off. OK then, take back the contract! Since he's not loved, he wants to die a soldier. Not only that, he'll never have peace of mind again...since the Doctor himself has fooled him! This finally proves to Adina that Nemorino indeed loves her. Her heart is filled with happiness.

"Oh! Inexpressible joy!" cries Nemorino, as he falls at her feet. The Doctor did not fool him after all!

Onto this scene marches Belcore with his men. What does he see? Arms are being presented to his rival!

"That's the way it is, Belcore...here is my husband..."

So what is done is done. Without so much as a sigh of regret, Belcore announces that it's Adina's hard luck...after all...the world is full of women—and thousands "want Belcore."

Dulcamara again interrupts about his elixir of love. Nemorino is really happy because of *him*. The crowd is struck with awe. Dulcamara doesn't stop there. Did they know that Nemorino is now the richest man in the village because his uncle died? Well, Adina and her new husband-to-be didn't know!

"I knew it...," sings Giannetta with the chorus.

"So did I," states the Doctor. "But what you don't know...is that this superhuman potion can instantly, not only cure love-sickness, but make the 'sick' ones *rich* as well!"

Everyone marvels at this "grand liquor." And since Dulcamara can't resist giving a pitch when he gets the chance, he goes into it once more to the same tune that he sang when he first came on the scene.

"It fixes any ailment...makes the ugliest creature

beautiful...helps the lame walk...makes swelling disappear..."

The peasants have got to have this precious liquid. They start to call for a bottle here, two there...three! And the Doctor goes on...

"...it gives courage to those young girls who are afraid to sleep alone! It's an awakener for lovers more powerful than coffee!"

He continues to have a very lively business...leaving them "a great treasure" that will give health, beauty, good-humor, luck and gold. While Adina and Nemorino admit that they owe their love and happiness to the Doctor...and Belcore good-naturedly wishes bad luck to the old fake...the cornet sounds once again as the Golden Wagon (or balloon) starts on its way. The cheerful voices of the villagers wish long life to the "grand Dulcamara" hoping that he will soon come back to them with his "treasure." Everyone is happy as four great chords mark the end of this most merry opera.

THE CURTAIN FALLS

And we are happy, too. Donizetti gave us a comic opera, true, but filled it with such wonderful lyrical music that the world has been enjoying its *bel canto* (beautiful singing) ever since. He gave us, too, some very moving moments that show how deeply real love can be felt.

Like Verdi, Donizetti also experienced tragedy in his private life. Only three years after *L'Elisir*, his wife, of a very short while—the elegant Virginia Vasselli, whom he adored—died. This, after all three of their children had died as infants.

Perhaps this is why Donizetti had that "rare quality" of being able to write funny operas as well as very tragic ones. And he wrote them almost as if he were two different people.

Although his next opera was the tragedy, *Lucia di*

Lammermoor, he went on to write more comic ones such as *The Daughter of the Regiment* and the hilarious *Don Pasquale*. So his ability to have fun never left him.

Looking back, we can imagine the fun he must have had at the opening of *The Love Potion*. As was mentioned, the soprano was a German, Clara Sabina Heinefetter; the tenor, Giovanni Battista Genero, had a stammer although he evidently could still sing; a Frenchman, Henry-Bernard Dabadie, played Belcore; and Giuseppe Frezzolini with "the voice of a goat" played Dulcamara. To make matters worse, the audience was impossible.

Hector Berlioz, a famous composer himself, was there that night. Here is what he had to say: "I found the theatre full of people talking in normal voices, with their backs to the stage. The singers...yelled their lungs out...at least I imagined they did, from their wide-open mouths...but the noise of the audience was so much that no sound could be heard but the bass drum."

Yet the opera was a hit...running for all of thirty-two performances! And it has been running ever since. It was performed in America for the first time on June 18, 1838, and sung in English at the Park Theatre in New York City. But it wasn't until January 23, 1904, that it opened at the Metropolitan starring the fabled Marcella Sembrich, Enrico Caruso, Antonio Scotti as Belcore, and Archangelo Rossi as the tall-talking medicine man, Dulcamara.

Gaetano Donizetti, born in Bergamo, Italy, on November 29, 1797, lived only fifty-one years, until April 8, 1848. In such a short time, he had given the world a huge wealth of music. He had been idolized and honored. (In Vienna, the Emperor himself titled him Court Composer and Master of the Imperial Chapel.) And, although he had become famous for his humor, his later years were tragic with sickness that finally brought his life to a close.

Toward the end he suffered from intense headaches. He was depressed; he "saw" things. Finally, at forty-five, he was found in his room, paralyzed. For the next year and a half he was in an insane asylum. Then, under his brother's care, he was again in Bergamo until his death. To the salute of gun-fire, in the light of thousands of torches carried by his townspeople, he was laid to rest.

Today, he stands with Rossini and Vincenzo Bellini as the opera world's brilliant threesome of the early 1800's.

Throughout this storybook we have traveled to many places in many countries. Once again we will go to a new land. But in this case we will not only be introduced to a different part of the universe...we will be brought into a whole new world of music: the world of a great genius—Richard Wagner (Rikard Vahg-ner). It's an interesting fact that the year 1813 marked the birth of two of the biggest musical giants who ever lived: Wagner, born in Leipzig, Germany, on May 22, and Verdi, born about five months later on October 10.

From the very beginning Richard Wagner was surrounded by disagreements, to put it mildly. During the spring of 1813, in the Kingdom of Saxony where he was born, there began the shooting of many cannons and muskets. Napoleon Bonaparte had again put together an army, and he was using Saxony as a jumping off place for the capture of Berlin. But on May 21 he was defeated in the battle of Bautzen...less than a hundred miles from where Richard was born on the very next day.

So Wagner grew up hating the French, among other things! His legal father, Karl Friedrich Wagner, weak from working hard and surrounded by the sick, the dead and the wounded, died of typhoid fever—only six months after the boy's birth.

His real father, the actor Ludwig Geyer, instantly took over. And, just as in today's soap operas, he married Wagner's widow Johanna not long after Karl died...and six months before a daughter Caclie was born to them.

If this seems confusing, you have some idea of how mixed up Richard Wagner's own life became. But in spite of all his affairs, his gambling debts and his early musical failures, he managed to come through with a "new music" that has been felt ever since.

He did all this even though he was not a nice person and was thoroughly disliked. He was selfish and ruthless. He used his friends only for what they could do for him, then threw them away. But he had the one thing that made him the giant he is today. He was sure that he was the greatest musician ever—the greatest writer of drama, the greatest poet, and the smartest man of his time! If it wasn't for this belief, he never would have survived all the rejection and criticism that he was bombarded with in his lifetime.

Finally, when things looked like they would never get off the ground, he got word from the young King of Bavaria, Ludwig II (who had become king at the age of nineteen), that he would set Wagner up so he could live in high style, and—more importantly—the King promised to pay for the staging of the works that had not been performed so far. And the first one to be put on was *Tristan und Isolde* at the National Theatre in Munich, June 10, 1865.

> *(To give you some idea of the "soap opera" quality of Wagner's life, here is a short note: While he was still living with his first wife [the former Minna Planer, an actress] in a home supplied by wealthy silk merchant Otto Wesendonck, he was "in love" with Otto's wife Mathilde. At the same time, he was finishing his "music-drama," Tristan. Then he met Cosima. She was the daughter of the famous composer and pianist, Franz Liszt, and the wife of Wagner's good friend, Hans von Bulow—also a pianist and conductor. It wasn't long before Cosima and Wagner "fell in love." By this time Minna was out of the picture—Mathilde, too. Then, since he was now a favorite of the King and about to stage Tristan, he had the gall to invite Von Bulow to play his operas at court. Cosima arrived eight days ahead*

of her husband, who was sick. Nine months later,
about an hour before the first rehearsal, Cosima
gave birth to Wagner's baby named—guess what—
Isolde! And believe it or not, Wagner was asked
to be godfather to his own daughter, with Von Bulow
and Cosima as the parents!

Some say that *Tristan's* passionate music was inspired by Wagner's love for Mathilde. Others, that he fell in love with her because he was writing *Tristan*. Whichever way it was, he did come up with a masterpiece. . .in which we see a "music-drama" and hear the "new music" he created.

The opera takes us now, by ship, to the shores of Cornwall, England, and the court of King Mark. It is the story that Adina was reading about a love potion that made a Cornish knight and an Irish princess fall madly in love. It is the tragic legend of. . .

3

Tristan und Isolde

(TRIS-tahn oond E-ZOHL-deh)

ACT I

Before the curtain rises we hear the *prelude*. Softly and slowly the music starts...cellos and oboes swelling until a full chord crashes. The violins sing of sadness and yearning. They almost disappear, then rise and sweep along, reflecting the unhappy spirit of the young girl being carried against her wishes to a strange land. We also hear a hint of the passions that will soon be bared— the whole orchestra filling the air with striving, with the force of love. The strings and woodwinds join in the lead theme (the *leitmotif*; the most important of Wagner's musical inventions) that will be connected with the two young lovers. Then all lightens and fades away.

We now see the sailing ship. Isolde is on a couch on the deck. She's in a separate area made especially for her. She's not happy. Brangane (Brahn-GAIN-eh), her servant, is looking over the side.

The strong, young voice of a sailor sings of the ship sailing eastward. . .with the fresh wind carrying him home. He asks "my Irish child" where she is roving—is it her sighs that keep the ship flying?

"Blow wind blow. . .sigh. . .my child!
Irish maid. . .you wild, darling maid!"

Isolde looks up with an angry start. Who dares to mock her? She sees Brangane and asks her where they are. The maid describes the sky. . .the sea is calm and they'll be landing before dark. It will be Cornwall! The girl loudly denies that she will ever go there! Brangane is worried. What does she mean?

But Isolde cries out that she no longer seems to have the power her mother gave her to control the sea and the storm. All she can do is put together some balmy potion. She wants once again the power to whip up storms. . .so that the ship will break into bits! We hear her violent thoughts in the music.

Brangane is alarmed. What has come over her mistress? She thought that something was very wrong when she noticed how coldly Isolde had left her mother and father, how she did not sleep or eat, how wild she looked. Won't the Lady Isolde please trust her? Won't she tell her what is torturing her? Her voice is tender.

But the spirited girl pays no attention. Instead she wants air. . .she feels shut in with all the curtains hanging around her deck space. Brangane quickly opens them and we see the full length of the ship. Tristan is standing there; Kurvenal (KOOR-ven-ahl), Tristan's faithful servant, is resting nearby. The sailors are busy with the landing of the ship.

Once again the young sailor sings his song about the "Irish child." His tone is sweet as he ends. But Isolde only has eyes for Tristan. Tragically, she looks at the one who has taken her from her homeland.

"What do you think of that hired man there?" she asks Brangane.

"Who do you mean?"

"That hero there...who can't look me in the eye...tell me, what does he seem like to you?"

Can her mistress mean Tristan...that unmatched hero? Isolde is scornful. She doesn't think he's so heroic...he avoids looking at her...he doesn't dare come near her. She orders Brangane to go to him and tell him to come to her...his mistress! It is her command!

The timid Brangane can't do anything but obey. She quickly approaches. Kurvenal sees her and warns his master that here comes a message from Isolde. Tristan is deep in thought, but this word startles him! Has he been thinking of the lovely princess?

"...My lady wishes you to come to her..."

Tristan shows a bit of his feelings when he comments that Isolde's trip must seem long, but it will soon be over. He will do whatever she wishes. Well, she wants him to go to her...now. But Tristan speaks of his duty to his king. Again Brangane tells him that her mistress wants him to go to her. The knight now gives the excuse that he is needed at the helm of the ship so that it will be safely delivered to King Mark. Brangane isn't fooled. If Tristan didn't understand her the first time, she'll spell it out for him. Isolde wants him to know that she's his sovereign and that he should fear her—Isolde!

Kurvenal can't take this anymore and wants to give the answer. "What will it be?" wonders Tristan. Kurvenal angrily tells her that a knight like Tristan can't be the "property" of someone who has been taken as a prize for the king. Especially not the great Tristan...even if there were a thousand Isoldes!

Brangane is insulted. She turns to go back. Tristan tries to keep Kurvenal quiet, but he, instead, starts to sing after her. He reminds her of when Lord Morold (the knight who was supposed to marry Isolde) came to Cornwall to collect the Irish tax. Tristan killed him in a duel! His bold voice ends as Tristan gets him to go below deck. Brangane angrily joins her mistress while the sailors take up Kurvenal's song.

The curtains are now closed again, shutting Brangane and Isolde off from the rest of the ship. The bitter girl is desperate. She wants to know what happened. She's having a hard time holding her temper. Brangane is excited as she tries to answer. Finally, she explains that Tristan said he could not come because he wanted to be sure to deliver the ship (and it's precious cargo) to King Mark.

In a high, angry voice, Isolde repeats this message. Her maid rushes along to tell her the rest, about Kurvenal. Isolde stops her. She heard everything only too well! Those sailors would not be so sarcastic if they knew how she had saved the wounded Tristan. The orchestra plays powerfully. Then her voice softens. There in a small boat this mortally wounded knight had arrived at the Irish coast. She, Isolde, used all her know-how...with salves and balms...to save the man who called himself, "Tantris."

He did not fool her for long. She saw that a splinter from his sword fit exactly the wound in Morold's head! She had swiftly raised that sword to avenge Morold's death! (Again we hear the thunder of the music.) But then Tristan looked up at her, not at the sword, not at her hand—but right into her eyes. She melted and the sword dropped from her hand. Then she healed him so that he would return home and no longer stir her with his glances! Her voice is quiet at the memory. Brangane, too, now remembers tending that strange knight. Then the mood changes.

In full voice Isolde cries about how Tristan is now hailed as a hero...when not so long ago he was at the point of death. The music sweeps upward.

> "He swore a thousand oaths...of thanks and faith! Now hear how a knight keeps his oath!"

Again Isolde thinks of how badly she's been treated for saving him. How he left her as the unknown "Tantris"—and came back as Tristan to get her for his uncle, King Mark. (Had she secretly hoped that Tristan would want her for himself?) She can't get out of her mind that instead of killing him, the sword just dropped from her hand. And this is the result! Her voice is light, thrilling. . .and then comes the crashing of the orchestra.

Brangane remembers how they were all so happy that peace had come to Ireland and England. Little did she know the misery that had been caused.

Isolde calls out her despair. . .at how blind everyone was. She had kept his secret. . .that it was Tristan who killed Morold. She had protected him from revenge. And the thanks she got was Tristan's coming back for her, by ways and roads that he knew. . .so that he could deliver her to his king! She hits a long note as she thinks of how he must have enjoyed this "adventure!" Now she loses control! She curses him! She cries for vengeance! For death! The horns in the orchestra sound. Then, desperately, she calls for both of them to die!

(Here, then, enters the love-death idea that Wagner created: In death they would be together forever. In death they would rejoice in their love.)

Brangane tries everything she can to comfort her mistress. She tries to show her that Tristan is really repaying her for her kindness to him. How? By getting her to be a queen! What more can she ask? After all, King Mark is noble. . .a prize.

All this doesn't touch Isolde at all. We now begin to see why. We know she actually is in love with Tristan. How can she stand being near him while all along she'll be married to somebody else? How can she bear that torture—not having her love returned?

"Where is there a man who would not love you?" comforts Brangane. "Who wouldn't love her at first sight?"

She reminds Isolde that she still has her mother's power. Yes, Isolde remembers. Revenge to those who betray. . .peace for the troubled heart. Now she gets an idea. She orders Brangane to bring her a small golden box. Inside are little bottles. Some to heal, others to protect against poison. (A hint of the love theme is heard.) Brangane holds up a love potion. . . the most precious of all. The desolate Isolde disagrees with her. She has marked the one for *her*! There are dark musical notes.

"The drink of death!" cries Brangane.

The voices of the sailors grow louder. They're getting the ship ready to land.

"How fast the trip was!" moans Isolde.

Suddenly Kurvenal strides in. He's full of pep as he tells the "women" to get up and get ready. Those at the castle know that Isolde's here by seeing the flag flying from the mast. So get ready to go with Tristan to meet the king!

Although both Brangane and Isolde are surprised at this boldness, the young girl is still a princess. It takes her only a moment to get back her pride. She wants Kurvenal to tell his master that she will only go with him if he first comes to her and asks her pardon. Kurvenal is about to say something when she stops him with her commanding voice. He is to give Tristan her message. . . and let him hope that she will forgive him!

"You can be sure he will be told. . ."

Isolde turns to Brangane. She takes her in her arms as she bids her farewell! Her voice is high. She wants Brangane to be sure to have all her friends remember her. . . to give her regards to her mother and father. Brangane is frightened.

"What's this? What are you thinking? Are you running away?"

No she's not. She's waiting for Tristan. She has a plan. . . a plan for them both. She wants Brangane to prepare the "drink of atonement." She shows her the one she means. Brangane is horrified. She is to fill the golden cup. The music follows as Brangane's voice climbs in protest.

Isolde declares that her mother would not have let her go to a strange land without being prepared with the magic potions. Some to heal wounds...some to ease pain...and for the deepest pain of all—*death*! Her voice soars as she calls for the drink of death. Then it takes on a dark tone as the drums rumble softly.

Will Brangane be "true" and do as she is told? Before she can answer, Kurvenal announces, "Lord Tristan!" Isolde proudly gives permission for him to enter. There's a heavy musical chord. Kurvenal leaves. Isolde is trying to get control of herself. Brangane is terrified as she retreats to the back. The princess can't tear her eyes from the place where Tristan will appear. The music is tragic with expectation...we hear the horns.

Finally, Tristan comes to the entrance and stands there. Isolde's eyes bore into him. Neither one has dared to realize that they are really in love. Isolde has been afraid to admit it to herself, yet her feelings are beginning to show. Tristan is held back by his loyalty to his king. He, too, doesn't fully know how deeply he's in love with this Irish girl who so tenderly nursed him back to health. What will happen to them? Is Isolde's idea of death for them both the answer? Again she can't bear the thought of being near Tristan and yet being married to someone else. Better to be dead than to be in a living hell. In death they will finally be together forever! In death they will have no one telling them what to do or not to do. In death they will find everlasting love! (This love-death idea is completely Wagner's. No trace of it is found in the original legend.)

"Command, Lady, whatever you wish."

Isolde wants him to make his peace with her for Morold's death. In a sense, to ask for her forgiveness. But first she gets back to why he has disobeyed her order to come to her. It was "obedience" (to his king) that kept him away. In his land it is the custom for the bride's escort to stay away from her!

Well, since he's all for "custom"...how about the one that says an enemy should be friendly.

"Who's the enemy?" asks Tristan.

She is, of course! But what about the peace that was sworn to by everyone?

"I did not swear...," declares Isolde, her voice ringing.

What she did swear was revenge for the death of Morold!

Did Morold mean so much to her, wonders Tristan? Is he trying to make fun of her? Morold was her husband-to-be.

"...for me he went to battle...and with his falling...so fell my honor..."

She had sworn then that if no man avenged his murder (her voice in full power) then she, a girl, would do it! Then her tone changes. She quietly reminds him that when he was sick and weak she could have killed him...but instead she cured him so that he would one day pay for the death of Morold!

"Since all the men are at peace, who will slay Tristan?" (The music thunders.)

"If Morold was so dear to you take my sword again and guide it to its mark...don't drop it again!" sadly answers Tristan.

But that's far from what Isolde has in mind. How would it look if the girl that was brought to be married kills the bridegroom's best knight? Besides, she is supposed to bring peace between King Mark and Ireland.

"Let us drink to forgiveness...," Isolde suggests, softly.

Meanwhile, she signals to Brangane to hurry with the poison! The sailors sing out the orders to land. Tristan is in a dream-world. Has he guessed Isolde's plan? Why is he so silent? Does he refuse to make peace? Again the sailors sing. At last, Brangane hands her the golden cup, filled to the top. Isolde brings it to where Tristan is standing. He looks deeply into her eyes.

"You hear the noise? We have landed." Isolde's voice is dark.

Soon they will both be there before King Mark. She paints the picture for him, to the sound of light violins. He will tell his king how he killed her lover and sent back his head, how she kindly healed Tristan's wounds...and, to the disgrace of her land (the music is getting louder), allowed her to be brought back to be bride and queen (her voice rises). Then, in thanks for all this (sarcastically), she made him a nice drink of peace...to wash away his guilt! Isolde ends, her voice climbing the heights!

"Out with the hawser! Drop the anchor!"

The loud sailors' voices snap Tristan out of his dreaminess. He starts to give orders to anyone who is listening.

"Drop the anchor! ...sail and mast up into the wind!"

He takes the cup from Isolde. Excitedly, with full orchestra, he tells her that he knows all about the witchcraft of "Ireland's Queen" (her mother). Watch him take his "pledge of peace." Tristan is also aware of his "endless sorrow"...when Isolde marries Mark. He, too, will take the only way out (he surely knows now that this is the drink of death)! He will take it gladly! And with that he starts to drink. Isolde sees that he's about to empty the cup. She grabs it from him. Is she going to be betrayed in this as well?

"Betrayer! I drink to you!"

The music explodes with sound! She drinks the rest and throws the cup away! But it isn't welcome death that arrives. Brangane could not bring herself to fill the goblet with poison. She could never be the cause of her mistress's suicide. Instead, she substituted a potion of love! We see the two young people changing before our eyes. Their glances meet, then are hidden—only to meet again. They can no longer help themselves. The music begins to shake, just as they are doing.

"Tristan...," Isolde's voice trembles at last.

"Isolde!" bursts Tristan.

She falls to his breast as his arms fold her to him with great passion. The love theme is heard. The drums get louder and louder. Gradually the orchestra brings forth the famous melody that exposes the enormous love that has been hidden inside of them.

"Hail! King Mark, Hail!"

The men's voices seem so far away. Brangane is in despair. She has saved them from death. . .but has she caused even worse trouble?

Tristan and Isolde don't know what has happened to them. Had he only dreamed of his "honor"? Had she dreamed of her "shame"?

"Isolde!"

"Tristan!"

"Most sweet maid!"

"Truest of men!"

Their duet grows into a wonderful expression of their love. They're throbbing. They're full of joy. Their voices join in glorious sound. The only thing that's real is their beautiful love for each other. (Even though the ship is now overrun with people.) Brangane is beside herself.

She quickly thinks of Isolde's royal robe. She rushes with it to get between them. She does manage to get the robe on, but Isolde doesn't even notice it!

"Hail! Hail! Hail! King Mark, Hail!

All hail King Mark!" sings the chorus, as cymbals clash and horns blare.

In strides Kurvenal. He hails Tristan. . .the great hero! He goes to tell him that King Mark is on his way, by barge, to claim his bride! But both lovers are thinking only of themselves.

"Who's coming?" asks Tristan.

"The king!"

"What king?"

Isolde, too, is in another world.

"What is it, Brangane? Why all the noise?"

"Isolde...Lady...be calm..."

"Where am I? I'm alive? Ha! What drink was that?"

Brangane can no longer hide the truth. Against her will she confesses.

"The love potion!"

Tristan and Isolde look at each other. The one thing they both had secretly dreaded was now a fact! Both of them in love...and she is to be married to another!

"Do I have to live...?" whispers Isolde, in his arms.

And while Tristan, too, thinks of how their love is over-shadowed by pain and treachery (to his king)...the cymbals clash again as the horns sound welcome to the King of Cornwall. The curtain falls.

ACT II

It is night. The garden is seen in its full summertime beauty. The orchestra opens with force, then flows into soft night music. Far off the sounds of hunting horns are heard. Brangane, fearful, is trying to see if the hunting party is really going away. A torch burns brightly beside Isolde's chamber door. The music twists and turns. The horns are still heard...as Isolde appears. She wants so much to have the hunters far away, that she no longer hears them. But Brangane does and tells her so. Silence.

The anxious girl insists that Brangane hears the horns only because she's worried. It's really just the sound of rustling leaves! But Brangane is not only worried, she fears a plot. Isolde hears what she wants to hear—Brangane still detects the sound of horns. Sure enough, there they are. The girl still argues. Her voice climbs as she wonders if Brangane's imagination is going to prevent Tristan from coming to her.

Brangane tries again. She describes how Melot—another of the king's knights—looked with jealousy and evil at Tristan as he turned over the unhappy bride to King Mark. She's seen him lurking about...planning a trap! So beware!

Of course, Isolde can't really believe that one of Tristan's most trusted friends would turn on him. Yet Brangane is troubled. She insists that the hunt was put together too fast. They are not off hunting game—but Tristan himself.

Isolde brushes off all this unpleasantness. She wants her maid to give the signal...her voice goes higher and higher...give the signal and put out the torch so her beloved will come to her! The full orchestra accompanies Brangane as she pleads with Isolde to leave the torch burning. She cries at the thought that she was the one who placed her mistress in such danger by giving her the potion.

As Isolde thinks of her love for Tristan, her voice becomes sweetly passionate. It was the goddess of love who changed her hate into love...who took away the cup of death and replaced it with one of love. She, Isolde, will do whatever she is "ordered" to do! The orchestra threatens. Brangane begs her to beware...not to let love blind her...to leave the torch burning.

But Isolde doesn't listen. Her heart is too filled with fire. She orders Brangane to go watch from the lookout tower. Then she boldly takes the torch herself and throws it to the ground!

In the darkness she impatiently peers deep into the garden. She can't stand it. She begins to wave her scarf. The music imitates the swaying of the scarf as Isolde signals faster and faster. She sees Tristan! The music gets louder and louder the closer he gets...and then full force as he appears.

From now till near the end of the act, it is one long love duet. Here, Wagner created some of the most sensually passionate love music ever composed. The lovers fall into each others arms.

"Isolde! Beloved!"

"Tristan! Beloved!"

Their voices are in the clouds!

"Are these your eyes?" cries Isolde.

"Is this your mouth?" wonders Tristan.

"Here your hand?"

"Here your heart?"

They can't believe that they are finally alone in each others arms. They never dreamed they could be so delirious. Neither one could wait for the torchlight to go out. Now they joyfully greet the blessed night...the darkness that hides them from prying eyes. Daylight is their enemy. They realize that they loved each other from the moment they met. Even though he was to win her hand for his king...he felt his love for her...yet he hid it from everyone. She, thinking that he did not love her...was ready to be joined with him in death! Instead, the doors of love were opened wide!

"O hail that potion!" calls Tristan. "Hail its powerful magic!"

Isolde can't believe that he is hers and she is his. Tenderly, she thinks about it all. Their "love-night" is being fulfilled. Gone is glaring day...with its lies. Only covering nighttime is worthwhile, where love will be forever true! The music captures this deep emotion. And finally, the wondrous love theme comes through as the heart of the duet is about to begin. It stays in the background as both sing...slowly and softly...

"Oh wrap around us, night of love...make me forget that I'm alive..."

If they are covered by the night, then everyday troubles disappear. All their fears fade away, as they lie there...

"Heart to heart, mouth on mouth...," whispers Isolde.

They are forever lost in one another. Their voices climb. They are in their own world...no more to awaken...only to live a life of love. Throughout the scene, waves of music rise and fall...pouring over them as their voices rise and fall as well. They are in heaven...but one that soon will end.

Far off, from her watchtower, Brangane's voice is heard warning them. In a gentle refrain she tells them to beware...as soon the night will fade away! Isolde hears her, dreamily. Tristan does not want to awaken. Even day will not kill their love. Or even death! In vibrant voice, Tristan defies death itself to destroy his love. His love is immortal...it can never die!

With a heavenly tone, Isolde thinks of how sweet their love is called—Tristan *and* Isolde. She wonders if death would not destroy the little word "and" that holds them together. Tristan assures her that even if they both should die, they would never be parted...they would be together forever..."never waking...never fearing...nameless...living on love alone!" Isolde repeats this thought, a little girl trying to understand. Then both, with voices strong, once again sing that they would live on love alone! Her head falls on his breast.

Again Brangane's voice is heard...warning, warning. Day is coming. Isolde rises to her feet. She hits a wonderful high note as she declares...

"May the night never end!"

Together they sing of "endless night...night of bliss..." How they would have no more fear...no more parting...alone together...nameless...always in love...always loving, loving, loving. The sounds are full and powerful, the violins are sweeping to a climax...upward, upward till they scream to a piercing end! Kurvenal suddenly enters with his sword drawn!

"Save yourself, Tristan!" He looks behind him.

It *was* a trap! In a moment, the treacherous Melot, the king and others pour onto the scene. They're amazed. All except Melot. He gloats to his king that he was right all along. He had bet his head that he was sure of Tristan and Isolde's "shame." The king is stunned. As the mournful bassoon plays, he asks if it is true, if his truest friend has really betrayed his trust. He wonders if Melot, after all, will be the one to avenge this wrong.

Tristan is not himself as he thinks he is seeing daytime ghosts in "morning dreams." He wants them to go away, to disappear!

But it is not a dream. King Mark, with deep sadness, asks. . .

"You, Tristan. . .have done this to me?. . ."

As the king continues to question Tristan's lack of faith, the knight's eyes fall and his face shows his sorrow.

Then King Mark laments. What good has all of Tristan's honor been if he now dishonor's his king? He remembers how he, the king, in thanks for all that Tristan had done for him, made him his heir. How, when his wife died childless, he thought of him as his only son. But the people—and Tristan as well—wanted him to have a true heir. . .wanted him to marry again. In fact, it was only because Tristan had said he would leave the court if he were not sent to bring his king a bride. . .that King Mark had finally agreed. And so it was that he went and asked a lovely girl. . .a princess. . .to come back with him. He brought back with him "a bride for a prince. . ." Now, he has wounded him to the heart. Why did he bring this shame on himself?

". . .secretly in the dark of night I had to sneak up on my best friend only to find the finish of my honor."

The violins play with excitement. Then softly, King Mark asks what it was that made Tristan commit such a harmful deed.

Tristan quietly admits he doesn't know. The love music is heard. He turns to his beloved. She looks up at him with longing. Will she now follow him wherever he should go? He doesn't mean to another land. He's really talking about death. . ."the wonderland of night." Will she follow him?

"Wherever Tristan has his home, that's where Isolde will be. . .that path now show Isolde!" Her voice flies to the skies.

Tristan goes to her and kisses her gently on the forehead. Melot is furious! He draws his sword!

"Traitor! Ha! Revenge, my King!"

Tristan can't imagine that anyone would dare challenge him.

He stares at the man who was once his friend...and because he, too, was overcome by Isolde's beauty, has now betrayed him! He draws his sword.

"On guard, Melot!"

Melot strikes at his enemy! But Tristan simply lets his sword drop. Melot's sword finds its mark—Tristan is terribly wounded! The music is now low...then, with a sudden burst, it stops! Kurvenal holds his master and friend in his arms as Isolde throws herself on her loved one. The curtain quickly falls!

ACT III

On the coast of Brittany, a section in the northwest of France, stands the castle of Tristan. There are turrets and a low wall, beyond is the wide stretch of sea. The castle is not well kept...it has seen better days.

There are only two figures in sight in the weedy garden. Tristan is lying there as if dead. Kurvenal is deep in despair as he tries to hear whether his master is still breathing. The music is soft and slow...gradually getting louder as the thin sounding violins take up an unhappy melody...louder and louder, slowly rising and falling.

From the distance, a shepherd's very sad musical piping is heard. Soon he appears at the wall and hails Kurvenal. He wonders if the wounded knight has awakened yet.

But Kurvenal shakes his head. He thinks that even if Tristan were to awaken, he would simply pass away. Only one person can heal him now. He asks the shepherd if he has seen anything of a ship across the sea. The shepherd assures him that if he had seen a ship, his tune would be happy, not sad. Again he wonders how the knight is doing. To the deep sound of the bass strings, Kurvenal impatiently advises him not to ask the same question. Just keep searching the "desolate and empty" sea, and if he should spy a sail then change to a bright, cheerful tune as a sign. Light violins play. The shepherd notes that the water is quite bare of a ship. He leaves and once again we hear the mournful piping.

To Kurvenal's surprise, the old melody awakens Tristan!

"Where am I?" he asks faintly.

Kurvenal springs to life to hear his master speak.

"...My lord! My Tristan!"

"Who calls me?"

"...new life is being given my Tristan!"

Tristan wonders if it is truly Kurvenal. He doesn't know where he was...or where he is. Why, he is in his family's castle— he's free and at peace in his castle, "Kareol." But Tristan is still not able to understand. He asks about the piping he has heard. A shepherd? His flock of sheep?

Kurvenal carefully explains that he does indeed own a herd...and the castle belongs to him, too...the castle that he left to his servants when he went off to foreign lands.

"To what land?"

"...Cornwall!" cries Kurvenal, to bright music, "where Tristan (his hero) won fame and fortune!"

"How did I get here?"

"...Well, he didn't ride back on a horse," says his friend.

Kurvenal, to the heroic sound of the orchestra, describes how he carried his master on his broad shoulders to a ship that took them home. Here in the sun of his homeland the bright rays will soon heal his wounds! But Tristan does not really think so. When he was unconscious he did not know where his spirit had gone. All he seemed to know was that it was where he wanted to be—in the darkness of night. Yet he could not stay there. He was "brought back" to daylight by his love for Isolde...his longing to see her again! His voice starts upward at the thought that he must once more face "accursed day"! He ends quietly as we again hear a hint of the familiar love theme. He wonders when there will be "night in the house."

Kurvenal tries to comfort him. He will see Isolde if she is still alive. The orchestra underlines his words. Weakly, Tristan says that Isolde is indeed alive—she had called to him out of the night! Kurvenal hurries to explain that he could think of only one "doctor" who could heal the wounds Tristan received from the traitor Melot, the same one who healed the wounds he had suffered from Morold. Isolde! So he had sent a trusted man to bring her back from Cornwall!

At this news the wounded knight finds new strength. Isolde is coming! He is overcome with joy at his Kurvenal, his true friend. How can he thank such great loyalty? What can he do to show how grateful he is? His voice climbs as he realizes that his faithful friend lives for him alone...suffers when he suffers.

Then he again speaks of his "terrible longing" for his beloved. He rushes along as he describes his feelings. He imagines the ship sailing to him...sails full with the driving wind. He is delirious as he thinks of Isolde flying to him. The flag on the mast is waving! The ship! The ship! In full voice he cries...

"Kurvenal, don't you see it?"

But just at that moment, the shepherd is heard still playing his sad song.

"There is still no ship to see...," says Kurvenal.

And as the piping continues in the background, Tristan slowly recalls how this same tune was played when his father died and later at his mother's death. Once again, it reminds him of longing for Isolde and of dying. His voice, along with the music, is powerful and strong. (It is the "heroic-tenor" voice that is so important to have when singing Wagner. Not many can be this *heldentenor*: a voice that is a rich baritone in the lower notes and yet must be brilliant and like a trumpet in the higher ones.)

In the gentlest of voices, he thinks of "Ireland's child." He goes over in his mind, once again, how she healed him...then wanted to poison him...and yet again, how they fell madly in love...all because of that drink! That drink that has filled his soul with so much yearning that he can hardly stand it! No amount of healing...no, not even death can free him from this passionate longing! His voice reaches the heavens. He quickly calls out against the boiling sunlight...the glaring light of day with all its torment. What he longs for is the peace and coolness of the all-hiding night! He reaches thrilling heights...the music ends with great power!

"I curse you...you awful drink! Curses on the one who made it!"

Kurvenal is shocked to see Tristan fall back. In a soothing voice, he calls to his hero...his Tristan. He tries to calm his unhappy and suffering friend. Sobbing, he wonders if he is dead. He listens for a breath. The music is silent. Then he sees signs of life! He sees Tristan barely moving his lips!

"The ship? Can you see it?" the faint voice asks.

"The ship? Of course, it arrives today...," answers Kurvenal.

Tristan can "see" it all. Isolde is there on board. She's waving. She's drinking a toast to their being at peace together. The violins play smoothly.

"Do you see? Can you see her yet?"

Tristan can. She's there...sailing to him...the gentle, noble girl. To a stirring melody, he describes the lovely Isolde.

He turns to Kurvenal. He wants him to go to the watchtower! Fast...fast...look for Isolde's ship—can't he see it? Kurvenal doesn't know what to do. But his answer is there in an instant! He hears the happy piping of the shepherd! It's true! Isolde's ship has been sighted! He rushes to the tower. There she is—coming from the north! In a high, thrilling voice, Tristan rejoices that he knew it all along. After all, his whole world is Isolde...how could she leave the world?

Kurvenal, too, is overjoyed. He sees the ship tacking, her sails full...cutting through the waves.

"The flag? The flag?" asks the anxious Tristan.

Yes, it's there...waving happily! Can Kurvenal see Isolde? Wait...the ship has disappeared behind some rocks. It's the reef! Tristan worries about the breakers rushing over the reef. Ships *have* been lost there. They wait. Is the helmsman a good one? The best. Maybe he's a friend of Melot! Tristan, in his grief, gets angry at Kurvenal. Well?

"Not yet...," cries Kurvenal.

"It's finished!" mutters Tristan.

Suddenly Kurvenal gives a shout! The ship has made it! They're through the treacherous reef! Tristan, in his happiness, grants all he owns to Kurvenal—the truest of friends!

"They're approaching at full speed!"

"Do you see Isolde?"

"She's there! She's waving!...With one leap she springs from the deck to the land!"

Through the joy of the music, we hear the heralding horns. Now Tristan wants his friend to rush down from the tower to the shore...to help her...help his woman! Kurvenal will bring her quickly...but he warns Tristan to stay where he is, resting on the couch.

Tristan is in ecstasy. He is to be joined again with his dearly beloved at last! He can't stand being in bed. His blood is racing. In his delirium, he trembles to his feet, tears the bandages from his wound and tries to stagger toward the castle gate.

"Tristan! Beloved!" cries Isolde from outside.

Tristan hears her...as his mind plays tricks.

"The torchlight, ha! The torchlight is put out! To her! To her!"

Isolde rushes in to where Tristan is weaving. The love theme is heard. They call to each other. But it is too late. With her name on his lips, Tristan sinks to the ground and dies in her arms. All is silent.

Isolde will not believe that he is gone. She's there. . .he must rise at her call. . .if only for just an hour. In a high voice, she pleads with him to "wake." She's longed to be with him again. . .for one short hour. Will he deny her this last moment of joy on earth? She wants to heal his wound so that they may be together for that night. But his eyes do not see. . .his heart does not beat! Her voice soars along with the sweep of the music. Why must she suffer so? Can't she tell him of her troubles? Just one more time?

Then she believes she sees Tristan awaken.

> "Beloved!" she cries in desperation, as she faints on his body.

All this time Kurvenal has been watching, speechless as he stares at the lifeless Tristan. Then the sound of men and arms is heard. The shepherd comes over the wall and warns Kurvenal that another ship has landed! He rushes to the ramparts. It's King Mark and Melot and their men! He calls to his own men to arm themselves with weapons and stones. The violins scream.

From below, Brangane calls to her Lady Isolde. Is she a traitor too, wonders Kurvenal? Melot and his men try to rush the gate. With one swing, Kurvenal strikes him dead! (The loyal Kurvenal does not understand. He believes Mark and the others have come in war. . .but, in truth, they have come in peace.) He fights on. . .and is mortally wounded! Mark is looking for Tristan. And Kurvenal, with his last breath, points to him.

> "He lies there. . .here. . .where I. . .lie. . ."

The king is torn with grief.

> "Tristan," he calls. "Tristan! Isolde! Woe!"

Kurvenal, too, calls to his master for the last time. He asks forgiveness. . .as he joins his Tristan. King Mark looks at them in sorrow.

> "Dead then, are they all! All dead! My hero, my Tristan! Most true friend!"

But Isolde has only fainted. Brangane suddenly realizes that she is coming to...that she lives! She hurries to explain that she had told the king the secret of the potion. He immediately sailed to find her and to set her free so that she could marry Tristan.

King Mark, too, explains how glad he was to discover that Tristan had not been guilty. Instead, he has only added to the misery by bringing more death and woe.

Isolde does not hear. Her mind is gone. She begins one of the most moving arias in all opera...the famous "Liebestod"— the "Love-Death" song. Sadly, calmly, as she gazes at Tristan, she imagines that he is smiling...that his eyes are opening. She is singing to the same music that filled the love scene in the second act. The mournful sound of a clarinet accompanies her. The orchestra seems to shake with emotion.

"...Friends...don't you see...him shining...carried high among the stars?"

Her voice rises and falls as she describes how "his heart...swells...and beats in his breast." She can feel his sweet breath coming from his lips. She calls on them all...asking them if they don't see the same things. Is she the only one? Her voice begins to weave as she becomes more and more emotional. She feels his breath swirling about her. Her voice lingers on every word...the music sweeping, driving...building to a full expression of her torment. All she wants now is to "sink into nothingness...without thought...the height of rapture!" The note is high and long...as the proud and lovely princess joins her Tristan forevermore. And as the violins weep, the full orchestra continues the beautiful, passionate, unhappy love theme...then softly fades away.

THE CURTAIN FALLS

Without question, Wagner changed the future of opera with *Tristan and Isolde*. His aim was to roll into one seamless ball

all the arts—music, language, drama—so that all would be united for the greatest possible effect. Although he did this in his works more than anybody else, it's the music that comes to the rescue when some of the other parts are not so strong. He gave the orchestra a place it hardly had before, which is why his music can be enjoyed so much, though nobody is singing. This adds to the fact that he wrote his own poetry to go with the music. He was his own librettist from start to finish!

In *Tristan*, Wagner did the best job of wedding all the arts into one piece. And he avoided his biggest faults—long-winded, boring and repetitive explanations of the story.

It took about three years for *Tristan and Isolde* to arrive at the Metropolitan Opera House after its opening in 1883...its American premiere taking place on December 1, 1886. One of the greatest singers of all time was Isolde, Lilli Lehmann. Her Tristan was Albert Niemann; Marianne Brant was Brangane; Adolf Robinson, Kurvenal and Emil Fischer, King Mark. Two greats of more recent memory were Kirsten Flagstad and the "Great Dane," Lauritz Melchior.

Not many are able to sing these parts...but as recently as 1974, at the Metropolitan, two "forces of nature" teamed up to give us an astounding, standing-ovation performance. It was Birgit Nilsson and Jon Vickers who treated the lucky audience to a fabulous night to remember!

Wagner went on to write one of the most stupendous compositions ever. It took him twenty-five years to complete the fantastic work called *The Ring of the Nibelungs*. This story about a magic gold ring includes dwarfs (the Nibelungs), giants, heroes, heroines, gods and goddesses. It's in four parts, each one needing a separate performance...with the last one taking five hours!

A whole new theatre had to be built just to put on *The Ring*. It stands today in the little Bavarian town of Bayreuth where (since the opening night of August 13, 1876) the work has been performed just about every year.

One of the main reasons that Wagner was able to do all this—besides his own stubborn and artistic nature—was that he finally found his true love in Cosima. She brought him the peace he needed to fulfill his dream. After three children, they were legally married in 1874.

All his life Wagner suffered from sensitive skin which was why he dressed in silks and satins and furs. In his later years, he also had stomach trouble, a swollen leg, and finally, a bad heart. He lived to see his dream realized. But then, at last, his heart gave out while on vacation in Venice. In the ancient palace of Vendramini-Calergi, his stormy life came to an end on February 13, 1883. He had gone to his room not feeling well. When his final attack took place, Cosima ran to him. A watch that she had given him had fallen to the floor; and as she held him in her arms, he died with the words "my watch" on his lips.

Today, he is buried in the garden of their home the Villa Wahnfried...only a few miles from where the Wagner Festival takes place. Cosima outlived him by almost fifty years, dying in 1930 at the age of ninety-two!

When we started talking about Richard Wagner, we noticed that in the year 1813 *two* musical giants came into the world. We already know quite a lot about Giuseppe Verdi because of the stories of *Forza* and *Traviata*. What we haven't touched on yet is what the two were doing at about the same time—age twenty-nine, thirty. Well, while Verdi won overnight fame with his *Nabucco* in 1842, Wagner went down to defeat with his *Flying Dutchman* in 1843.

But that, of course, didn't stop him. Two years later he put on *Tannhauser*. This didn't catch on either until, little by little, it began to grow on people. Some thought it was obscene; singers thought it was hopeless to try to sing it. Three years after that Wagner finished *Lohengrin*, which was not performed until 1850. But Wagner didn't get to see it until eleven years later!

Because he was angry at a society that didn't like his new music, he became a revolutionary. And when the revolution fizzled, he had to run to keep out of jail. During those years both operas began to be appreciated. At the same time, he was beginning to think about his big work, *The Ring*. He started to write articles against the style and form of Italian opera! In effect, then, he was in direct opposition to Verdi.

Meanwhile, Verdi had produced fourteen operas, and by 1850 had established himself as the revolutionary voice of freedom. He was getting near to what is known as his "middle period"— the time of *Rigoletto*, *Il Trovatore* and *La Traviata*.

We can only thank heaven that both geniuses were busily at work in their own worlds creating music that can be enjoyed by all. And so, as we leave Wagner deep in his efforts to build his most impressive work, let us turn to the two Verdi operas that together with *Traviata* make up the triple blockbusters of the opera scene.

Verdi had been asked by the opera house in Venice to write another score. He and his librettist, Francesco Maria Piave, started to look around for a good story. Piave knew by now what kind would fire up the "Maestro" since he had already written five earlier operas for him. After a while, the one that caught Verdi's imagination was a play written by the leading French playwright, Victor Hugo, called *The King Amuses Himself* (*Le Roi S'Amuse*).

Right from the start he was in trouble with the Austrian and Italian censors. Hugo's play was about a real king, Francis I, of France. He was quite a ladies man, to say the least, having had affairs with the daughters and wives of his own men of the court. One was Diane de Poitiers whose father, Saint Vallier, put a curse on the evil king.

But the character that really sparked Verdi was a hateful and hating crippled hunchback! (Was this another Quasimodo, the famous Hunchback of Notre Dame, whom Hugo had created the year before?) In a sense we could say so. . . for, like Quasimodo, who loved the gypsy girl, the jester Triboulet had one good streak—his love for his only daughter. With Verdi, he became one who could be pitied.

So Verdi had to argue with the censors about showing a rotten king as well as an ugly, scornful court jester who was helping the king in his affairs!

He started to get around all the problems by changing the King of France to a Duke of Mantua (a small Italian city). However, although he made other little changes, he wouldn't give up the figure of Triboulet. To him he was "a creation worthy of Shakespeare"—and for Verdi there was no higher praise. He also was carried away with the idea of the curse. In fact, at the start, he was calling the opera *La Maledizione* (The Curse). But later, the hunchback won out. Verdi himself said that the idea of a character that looked "ridiculous and deformed" outside, yet was filled with passion and love inside, was "superb."

From Triboulet the name was Italianized to Triboletto. But then, since all the other names of the play had been changed, the name became finally, Rigoletto. (Some believe this came from the French word "rigoler" which means to make fun of or to jest.)

At last, the night of March 11, 1851, arrived. All Venice was going to the opera house, La Fenice. . . and all Venice would hail the first Verdi opera that would make him world famous! From "freedom music" which had made him a hero in Italy, he now had written music of human passions and love.

Victor Hugo had given the world a play with new freedom (he believed the stage should be able to treat the ugly as well as the beautiful), new life and energy. And Verdi answered with an opera that was not made up of just a number of arias. . . but where the drama and the music were more closely united to become a tense, driving force from beginning to end. (Remember Wagner?) Yet the Verdi touch. . .the beauty of melody that is his alone, is there all the way through. . .giving us hours of joy that are never forgotten.

With that, let's go to the Mantua of the 1500's and see what happens to the unhappy, tragic jester known as. . .

4

Rigoletto

(Ree-go-LET-to)

ACT I

There is a short bit of music that gives us a feeling of what
is to come. Soft horns are heard...a sudden burst of
sound...then back to soft horns. The melody is repeated...and
soon gets louder and louder, more and more excited until it ends
in another burst. From a fanfare of horns, the music is picked
up by violins that cry in pity. Once more the horns play
softly...kettle drums grow louder up to a final flare.

A lively party is in full swing. The Duke's palace is bright with
lights; guests are in the back rooms, others are arriving. The
spritely music pictures the gala scene.

The Duke is heard talking to one of his courtiers, Borsa. He's hoping to finally "end his adventure" with that beautiful girl he's been seeing in church. It's been three months that he's been looking at her and following her home to see where she lives. He mentions a mysterious man that enters there every night.

As some ladies and their escorts walk across the scene, Borsa notices how much beauty there is—"just look!" The Duke, who doesn't need anybody to tell him about gorgeous women, claims that "the winner" is surely the wife of Count Ceprano (Cheh-PRAH- no).

"Don't let him hear you," warns Borsa.

"What do I care?"

Well, the story may get around...especially if one of the other women hears about it. That wouldn't be very good, thinks the Duke; he wouldn't want any of them to believe that he's a one-woman man!

And into one of the opera's many wonderful melodies he goes.

"This one or that one...to me they're all the same..."

His heart doesn't favor one "beauty" over another. If one likes him today, tomorrow there'll be another! Faithfulness...is terrible, cruel, since it puts a limit on love. You can't have love without freedom. Forget angry husbands...or lovers...even if a hundred eyes were looking at him, he'd still go after any beauty that struck his fancy!

The music now begins a minuet as the ladies and gentlemen of the court start to dance. While this is going on, the Duke stops the Countess.

"You're leaving? Cruel one!"

"I have to go with my husband."

Not wasting a minute, the Duke starts smoothly telling her what a sparkling beauty she is. Everbody's heart must be beating for her. His is already drunk, conquered and destroyed by the "flame of love." The Countess is embarrassed...he must calm down! She takes his arm as they walk out of the ballroom.

All this hasn't escaped the Count's eyes. Seeing this, Rigoletto, smirking, goes over to him.

"What have you got in mind, Sir Ceprano?"

But the angry husband turns furiously and follows his wife. This delights Rigoletto...and the others. Borsa leads them in commenting that the Duke is—even here—having a flirtation.

"Isn't he always that way?" cries Rigoletto smugly.

"Gambling, wine, galas, dancing, battles...he likes them all!"

Then, noting that the Duke must be doing well in his affair with the Countess, judging from her husband's rage, he follows them out.

That's what Marullo (Mah-ROOL-oh) has been waiting for! He's got great news about Rigoletto! What? Has he lost his hunchback? Isn't he crippled any more? They all joke at these ideas. No...it's even stranger than that. That crazy has...Well?

"A lover!"

"A lover! Who'd believe that?"

"The hunchback has turned into a Cupid," laughs Marullo.

"That monster? Cupid?" wonders the chorus.

Just then the Duke and his jester come back. The Duke is all aglow about Ceprano's wife...she seems like an angel to him. Rigoletto pushes him along. How about tonight? What about the Count? Prison? No! All right...exile! The Duke stops Rigoletto's dumb ideas.

"All right then...his head...," suggests the jester.

Just at that moment, back comes Ceprano! He's heard Rigoletto..."that black soul!" The Duke gets into the spirit of the thing.

"Did you say *this* head?" he laughs, tapping Ceprano.

"It's only natural! What's he doing with it? How much is it worth?'' sneers Rigoletto.

This enrages Ceprano! He's going to run his tormentor through with his sword, but the Duke stops him. Rigoletto only laughs. . .he's sure of his protection. The chorus sees Ceprano's fury.

The Duke takes Rigoletto to one side and criticizes him for always pushing things too far. Now everyone starts to talk at once. It's one of those amazing Verdi combinations where, to a lively melody, all the voices sing about their own thoughts.

Ceprano wants to get even with Rigoletto. He, in turn, is telling the Duke that he's not afraid. The Duke is bawling him out for getting himself in hot water. Borsa, Marullo and the rest want to know from the Count how they can get back at Rigoletto. After all, he's been a pain to them all. They swear revenge. . .and tonight's the night! They all agree to meet to take care of that crazy jester once and for all!

To change the mood, the Duke and Rigoletto turn back and sing that everything is "joy". . .everything is a "ball!" The others join in. . .and all end up on a high, happy note. . .even though they don't really mean it! They are just about finished when in walks Count Monterone (Mohn-teh-ROH-neh)! He wants to speak to the Duke. Rigoletto mocks him and imitates him. He accuses Monterone of plotting against them. . .but they will be kind and pardon him. This is not the time to bring up his daughter's honor! The jester laughs at him. Monterone becomes more and more angry.

(Now comes the spark that lights up Rigoletto's mind. . .the thing that he cannot forget—even at the very end.) Monterone threatens the Duke. He will destroy him. . .and avenge the insult to his family. (The violins pick up the mood, as they play in the background.) And if he is executed his ghost will return with his head in his hand. . .to cry out revenge from heaven and earth!

The Duke will hear no more—he orders him arrested! Rigoletto calls the Count a madman. The courtiers also believe he is insane. But Monterone continues to curse them all; turning directly to the hunchback, he puts a curse on him.

> "...And you, snake, you who laugh at a father and his troubles...you are accursed!"

The orchestra is silent...then in a roar, it crashes over the scene. Rigoletto is terrified. He can't believe his ears. The Duke now has an excuse to get rid of the old Count. He has to pay for breaking up the party. It was a deadly hour for him...to have spoken the way he did. (There is a mumbling of voices from the courtiers.) Rigoletto is still horrified by the curse. And to make matters worse, Monterone repeats it...while the Duke and the others say again that all hope for him is gone! As the orchestra closes with six deep chords, the poor Count is led away by armed guards. The act ends.

When Verdi has Monterone curse Rigoletto for laughing at a father whose daughter has been shamed, he brings up again the father-to-children theme that he wrote into at least fifteen operas that come to mind. (Father Germont in *La Traviata*.) No doubt it was a subject very dear to his heart. Could it have been because of his own sorrow at the loss of his young children? Surely that must have affected him greatly. Although he married again years later, he never had another child. But his operas speak of the deep fatherly love he felt inside. We shall soon see how this love is beautifully treated in the acts that follow.

ACT II

It is night and Rigoletto, muffled in his coat, is making his way home. He is still muttering about the old man's curse! He has almost arrived when a shadowy shape calls to him.

> "Sir!"

> "Go away...I've nothing to give you."

But it is not a beggar—it is a man with a sword!

"A robber?"

"A man who, for a little money, will get rid of an enemy—and you have them..."

In the background a swaying melody keeps them company. Rigoletto is interested...especially when the murderer mentions that he knows of "his lady" in the house! He asks how much it would cost to kill a nobleman. That would be a bit more. Half to be paid ahead of time...the rest when he's dead. Where? Well, in the city...or at the killer's house. There it's easy since he has a sensuous sister who lures them inside. One stab and he dies!

"I understand," murmurs Rigoletto, thinking of what a devil the man is.

"No noise..."

"I understand."

"Here's my blade. May it serve?"

"No, not at the moment!"

"Too bad..."

"Who are you?"

In a high, but quiet, voice the assassin answers: "Sparafucile (Spah-rah-foo-CHEE-leh) is my name!" He's from Burgundy...and can be found in the same place every night. Rigoletto now asks him to leave. As they part, he repeats his "go...go" (while Sparafucile darkly repeats his own name...finally disappearing from sight) to the sinister sound of the bass cello. The jester looks after him sorrowfully.

He begins to think...and in a passionate aria he bitterly realizes that he and the murderer are very much alike.

"We are both the same! I use my tongue; he uses his knife. I make them laugh; he stamps out their life! (Oh, that old man cursed me!)"

He's tortured by the idea that both "man and nature" have made him a vile wretch! Hunchbacked! A fool! All he can do is laugh—he isn't even allowed to find comfort in tears! (We begin to see a hopeless, pitiful man.)

He thinks of his master: young, playful, powerful, handsome. He's forever ordering him to make him laugh. Damnation! Those rotten courtiers...how they delight in making a fool of him. Then, to the sweet sound of the violins, he reflects that they have made him what he is...and that right on the spot he will change! Once again he thinks of the curse. Why is that thought always on his mind? Will it bring him bad luck? He shrugs it off.

"Ah, no! That's foolishness!"

And, as the high violins take up the same quick melody of the first act, he hurries through the garden gate of his home.

As he goes into the garden, his teen-age daughter runs to him. She's very happy to see him as he holds her in his arms. Gilda (Jeel-dah) knows how much he loves her. She is his whole life. Without her he would not have anything "good" on earth. Gilda notices that he is troubled. Why does he sigh like that? (The music starts a quick tune as they speak.)

He has kept her so hidden away that she wonders why all the mystery. She wants to know more about her family. He sharply answers that she has none! She pouts that if he doesn't want to talk to her...But he interrupts.

"Have you gone out?"

"Nowhere but church."

"That's good."

Now she starts again. If he doesn't want to talk about himself...at least won't he tell her about her mother? In a melodious way, he remembers how her mother—"that angel"— felt sorry for him...loved him because she pitied him. He cries at the thought of her dying—leaving her daughter as a comfort to him. He thanks God for that!

Gilda realizes how much pain her father must have felt. Her heart aches for him. She wants him to stop his bitter tears. He tells her over and over that all he has in life is her. All she has to know is that he is her father. As for others, they only wish him bad luck.

What about his country...his family...his friends? No...his whole world is Gilda. She asks why she has not been allowed to see the city...even after she's been at the house for months. She doesn't know that Rigoletto dreads the idea that someone could follow her home and take her from him. They would think it's a fine joke to play on a lowly jester! He calls out to Giovanna (Gee-oh-VAH-nah) the maid.

"Sir?"

"Did I see someone?" asks Rigoletto, suspiciously.

"Ah, no, no one."

"That's good...Is the door...always closed?"

"Always...always..."

"Listen...tell me the truth..."

"Always..."

His voice turns loving as he warns Giovanna to take good care of "this flower..."

Suddenly we see the Duke (dressed as a student) sneak into the garden. He sees them and quickly hides. No one has spotted him.

Gilda complains that her father always has some new suspicion. But Rigoletto (to the sound of violins and the soft rumble of drums) still asks the maid if she is sure no one has followed them from church. Never!

Meanwhile, the Duke has recognized Rigoletto!

"If anyone knocks...guard against opening."

"Even if it's the Duke?"

"Especially him!"

Rigoletto turns to leave and bids his daughter farewell. The Duke is shocked to hear that Gilda is actually his jester's daughter!

"Good-bye, my father...," sings Gilda.

In a slow, flowing duet Rigoletto repeats his warning to Giovanna to guard well his innocent child. Over and over he asks that she watch "this flower." Gilda can't understand why he is so fearful. She tries to calm him.

"There in heaven, near God, a guardian angel watches over me..."

Then, at the end of the duet, with the words "Father, my father...goodbye!" she hits the stratosphere...as Rigoletto finally leaves.

But Gilda *has* been followed from church! She worries about not telling her father. Giovanna asks whether she likes this young man. When she answers that she thinks he's handsome and that he seems to be in love with her, we hear a touch of the famous aria that is soon to come.

Her maid mentions that he looks like a "lord." Oh, no. Gilda sings a lilting tune. She doesn't think that he is a lord or a prince. She feels that he is poor...which makes her love him all the more. Her young heart is really dazzled by the thought.

"Asleep or awake...I'm always calling him...And my soul, in ecstasy, tells him that I lo—"

She's interrupted by the Duke who can't hold back. (He had already signaled the maid to leave!)

"I love you! I love you!" finishes the Duke.

He wants her to repeat those tender words.

Gilda is in a panic. She calls to Giovanna, but she has disappeared. She despairs that no one hears her. The Duke replies that *he* is there...but the girl is afraid. Who is it who wants to meet with her? It doesn't matter whether it's an "angel or devil...I love you!" She wants him to leave.

"Leave! Now! Just when the flame of love is about to flare!"

He goes into a gentle love song.

"...love alone is life...the voice of love is the beating of our hearts...so love me, heavenly lady, and I will be the most envied of men!"

Gilda is swept off her feet. These are the sweet words that she had dreamed about. She joins him in song. She repeats her dream of love...as he begs her to love him in return. Their voices slowly come to a close. The Duke insists that she tell him again that she loves him. The shy girl reminds him that she has already said so. She wants to know his name.

In the shadows outside the house appear Ceprano and Borsa! This is the place! Good. They creep away. The Duke now gives his name. Walter Malde. He's a student—and poor! Before he can go on with his lies, Giovanna hurries in. She has heard footsteps! Gilda wonders if it is her father returning. (The Duke wants to get his hands on the "traitor" who is spoiling his act.)

The frightened Gilda orders Giovanna to have the Duke quickly leave by the gate. He's slow to go and wants to know again if she loves him. What about *him*? He will love her for life! Before he can go on, the young girl—who is very troubled—insists that he speak no more...that he go at once. Together...in a *cabaletta*...they sing their good-byes. On a final high note they swear that they live only for each other. Then Giovanna quickly shows the Duke out.

Gilda is alone. The night is quiet, peaceful. She is thrilled with her new (and only) love. The music begins one of the most sensitive *coloratura* arias ever written. She is overcome at knowing his name. The name of her lover...Almost breathlessly she sings and the flute keeps her company with its breathy lowest notes.

"Dear name...to which my heart gave its first happy throb...will always remind me of the delights of love... Through my thoughts, my desire will forever fly to him

...and until my last breath (her voice soars) to me it will always be a dear name..."

She begins to leave the garden to go to her bedchamber. But once again she calls that beloved name. Her voice gives a quivering trill. At last, with his name still on her lips, she enters the house...and we hear her voice in the distance again lovingly repeating "Walter Malde."

A group of masked men show up in the street. They have seen the girl and are struck by her charm and beauty. This, then, is Rigoletto's love! What a beauty!

At that moment, along comes Rigoletto. He's heard some laughing. Who could it be? He wants to know who is in the shadows. Marullo comes out and identifies himself. It's so dark nothing can be seen. When Marullo reveals that they are all there to kidnap the wife of Count Ceprano, Rigoletto breathes a sigh of relief. How will they get in? Why, with this key, of course. They hand the jester the key. This again makes him feel better— at least they are not entering *his* house. When Marullo mentions that they are all masked, Rigoletto agrees to put on a mask too. What he doesn't know is that when they mask him they tie it on with a bandage which makes him blind as well as hard of hearing! They can barely keep from laughing as they get Rigoletto to hold the ladder against his own wall!

A lively chorus of hushed voices warns everybody to be quiet as they go to get revenge on "Ceprano." (But the Count himself is one of the kidnappers!)

"Quiet, quiet, quiet...quickly, quickly, quickly... We'll steal away the lover, and tomorrow the whole court will laugh!"

Some of the men go into the house and return swiftly carrying Gilda gagged with her scarf. As they hurry her away, the scarf falls off and she wildly cries for help from her father. The poor jester is so bandaged up he cannot hear. The violins sound, then the full orchestra.

"They haven't finished yet!...What a laugh!"

He impatiently touches his "mask," and to his horror discovers the trick. He tears it off. A lantern that the men left behind shows him where he is. There's Gilda's scarf! (The first violins now set up a repeated strain; they become louder and louder as the terrified Rigoletto tries to speak to Giovanna but cannot.) Finally, desolate, he calls to his daughter—"Gilda! Gilda! Gilda!"—but all is silent. Then in a choking voice he remembers...

"Ah!...*The curse!*"

And with the music reflecting the tragic scene, Rigoletto falls to the ground...as the curtain falls as well.

ACT III

To a brisk violin introduction, we find ourselves back in the Duke's palace. It is his private rooms. He comes in hurriedly and we can see he's very troubled.

"She has been stolen from me! But when...? In a moment...even before I was able to follow my own suspicions...! The door was open...and the house deserted! And where is that dear angel now? The one who awakened true love in me for the first time?"

He will get revenge on those who have made his dear one cry. Then, in a lovely waltz melody, he imagines that he can see her tears running...from her lashes...can hear her call his name as she remembers their love...in her moment of sudden danger.

"And I could not help you...my dearly loved girl..."

His sadness at the loss of Gilda is interrupted by her kidnappers rushing in.

"Duke, Duke! We've stolen Rigoletto's lover!"

"Really? How? Where?"

"Right from his house!"

"Ah! Tell me how?"

The Duke seats himself to hear the story. There's a fanfare. Then all the courtiers start a catchy tune and describe the whole affair. The lies about the Countess. The blindfold. The ladder. The escape. It's suddenly clear to the Duke that they are talking about his beloved! The men are gloating and gossiping about their success. . .when in comes the jester. (The violins cry their introduction of poor Rigoletto.)

He is a broken man. He can hardly keep on his feet. He also knows that he must put on an act. In a halfhearted way he tries to show them that he doesn't care. He sings a sorry "la ra, la ra, la ra." Marullo calls him "poor Rigoletto." The others bid him good day.

"Have they all been in on it?" he asks himself bitterly.

"What's new, clown?" Ceprano asks scornfully.

"What's new, clown?" imitates Rigoletto. "Whatever it is that's making you more sickening than usual."

As everyone laughs, Rigoletto continues his humming. He's looking everywhere for a sign of Gilda. He wonders where they have hidden her. The rest are tickled at the jester's misery. He turns to Marullo. He's glad to see that the night air hasn't bothered him.

"This night?" asks Marullo innocently.

"Yes. . .Oh it was a beautiful stroke!"

"I've been asleep."

"Ah, you were sleeping. Then you must have dreamed," Rigoletto spits out hatefully.

Painfully, he walks here and there. He still hums as he picks up a lace handkerchief from a table. The courtiers are watching him closely. Sadly, the jester sees that it is not his daughter's. He asks if the Duke is still asleep. Yes, he is still sleeping. Before another word is said, a page comes in with a message.

It seems that the Duchess wants to speak with her husband. "He's asleep. He's out hunting." The page is confused. How can he be doing that without pages or weapons? The courtiers are trying to keep him quiet by telling him anything but the truth. Especially with Rigoletto there.

"Don't you understand that at this time he can't see anyone?"

This now tells Rigoletto what he wants to know! His Gilda is here. She's with the Duke. She's there behind that door! The courtiers brush him off by suggesting that if he is looking for his mistress, he better search somewhere else. He looks at them in amazement. Then with his voice filled with scorn and sorrow he throws at them the truth.

"I want my *daughter*!"

The orchestra adds a thunderbolt of sound. His daughter! They're all surprised and shocked!

"Yes, my daughter...what a victory...What? Aren't you laughing now?"

She's in there with the Duke and her father wants to get her back. The men still stand in his way. This, then, is too much. He becomes furious. To the violins and a powerful, steady rhythm of sound...Rigoletto turns on them all.

"Courtiers, a vile race that's damned...for what price did you sell my loved one? You would do anything for gold. But my daughter is a priceless treasure."

Still trying to get into the other room, Rigoletto threatens them with the strength of a father whose daughter's honor he's striving to defend. He demands that these "assassins" let him open "that door." A heavy musical chord bursts out. Then to a repeated beat, Rigoletto (in tears) pleads with Marullo to tell him where they have hidden her. No answer. In a suffering voice he asks them all to forgive him...to have pity and return a daughter to an old man.

"A daughter who is the whole world to me..."

Finally, with a high, long note he begs, for the last time, for them to have pity on him. And as the crippled jester melts into tears...with the music suddenly taking on a hurried beat...the door flies open and Gilda rushes into her father's arms!

Rigoletto is overjoyed to have his daughter back. She is his whole family. He tries to comfort the trembling girl. And as he looks up again to those around them he hopefully says that it was all a joke..."isn't that true...isn't that true?" Then why is she crying?

He starts to be alarmed. She can't tell him why unless she is alone with him. He orders the men to go...and if the Duke comes this way...they should tell him not to enter! They decide not to argue with "children and madmen." They leave them alone. Silence. To a touching melody, the frightened girl starts her story.

"At all the feast days...while praying to God in church...a handsome young man caught my glances...and although our lips were silent...our hearts spoke through our eyes..."

Then this "poor student" came to meet her in the night...and expressed his "ardent love." When he left her heart was full of hope. Then her voice rises with excitement as she tells how strange men came and cruelly snatched her away!

Her father moans that he brought all this on himself...from his own actions, his daughter became the victim. In a mournful duet, he calls to her to "weep...little girl...weep...let your tears flow on my heart..." Gilda is grateful to him for helping her...for being a "comforting angel." The strings weep with them as their voices flow higher and finally come to an end.

Rigoletto decides that he will take care of what little he has to do and then they will leave this terrible place forever. Just as he is muttering at how one single day has changed everything, the doomed Count Monterone is seen being taken to prison. He stops in front of a picture of the Duke.

"Since my curse did not work...and no lightning or sword

has struck your breast. . .you will go on living happily. . .Oh, Duke!''

He slowly goes away with his guards. The jester takes a long look after the doomed man. Then, in a voice filled with bitterness and anger, he sweeps into an aria that has such a powerful rhythm that the tension builds and builds until its final climax. The old man Monterone is mistaken. . .he *does* have an avenger!

"Yes, vengeance. . .a huge vengeance is the only desire of my soul. . .Like a bolt of lightning from God. . .the clown knows how to strike!''

And while Gilda begs her father to forgive and forget, he repeats his vow of ''vengeance. . .like a bolt of lightning from God. . .the clown knows how to strike!'' With his voice reaching new heights, and Gilda trying once more to change his mind, the emotional duet comes to a tremendous end!

ACT IV

The scene opens to low, fearful music. It is night. In a lonely spot, alongside the Mincio River, a broken down inn is the home of Sparafucile and his sensual sister Maddalena (Mah-dah- LEH-nah). Because it is so run down, Gilda and her father can easily see through the cracks at what happens inside.

There is a problem.

"And you love him?" murmurs Rigoletto.

"Always!"

He doesn't know what to do. How does he solve the puzzle of a woman's heart? He insists on revenge even though his daughter is asking him to have pity.

"And if you were sure that he was unfaithful, would you still love him?"

"He's not. . .he adores me."

"Him?"

"Yes," she answers stubbornly.

"All right, then look here."

When Gilda peers into the inn, she only sees Sparafucile; but then the Duke comes in dressed as a cavalry officer! She's stunned. She hears him order a room and some wine—that's the way he always starts. The assassin leaves.

Now begins an aria that is probably the most familiar of them all. (Verdi knew what he had and was so sure that it would be a terrific hit that he didn't give it to the tenor to sing until the last minute. And even then, he warned him about it. "Be careful...swear that you won't let anybody see or hear the melody of this little song. Don't hum it, don't whistle it...It's so easy to remember that anybody could steal it...and then goodbye! They would be singing it all over...Venice...before the performance.")

"A woman is as flighty as a feather in the wind...changeable in what she says and what she thinks. Always with a pleasant face...whether crying or laughing...she is still lying. He is always miserable who gets attached to them... Who confides in them...doesn't do his heart any good! No one can feel really happy if he hasn't tasted from the cup of love!"

Again he sings of the "flightiness" of women...so changeable in everthing they say and think! He ends on a wonderful high note, as Gilda listens hopelessly.

When Sparafucile (which means gun-shooter) comes in with the glasses and wine, he taps on the wall to get his sister to show up. Then he sneaks outside to plot with Rigoletto.

"There's your man...does he live or die?"

Rigoletto can't tell him yet, since he has not been able to change Gilda's mind. The murderer strolls away.

The Duke starts to make love to the gypsy girl. Gilda can't believe her eyes. She can't believe that he is telling that girl the same things he had said to her! He continues to carry on with Maddalena who is playing hard to get.

"You're drunk!"

"With passionate love!"

He even says he wants to marry her! She demands that he give his word of honor...to make sure he means it.

Outside the father and daughter are still listening.

"Isn't that enough for you?" Rigoletto asks.

"The traitor...," admits Gilda.

Now is the moment that brings an audience to its feet. It is the spectacular quartet where Verdi, by using different rhythms, makes the different feeling of four voices completely understandable! No one has ever written a better quartet.

It begins with the Duke's voice telling of his "love" for Maddalena.

"Beautiful daughter of love, I'm a slave to your charms; With only one gift...you can ease my pains. Come and listen to the rapid beat of my heart..."

Maddalena isn't easily fooled. She knows he's just playing a game. Gilda is crushed; she sobs her despair.

"He said the same things to me..."

"Quiet...it's no use crying," comforts her father.

And so it continues. The Duke up to his old tricks...Maddalena playing along with his game ...Gilda crying at seeing her dreams of love shattered...Rigoletto trying to stop her tears as he reminds her of the Duke's lies. He knows the "remedy"...he will get his revenge!

As soon as this marvelous blending of voices comes to a close, Rigoletto turns to Gilda. She must listen to him. She is to return home and dress up as a young man, ride off to Verona...and he will be there the next day. Gilda is afraid to leave. She wants him to go with her. (She's worried about what he might do.

Despite everything, she still does not want the Duke killed.) But her father insists and Gilda obeys.

He meets with Sparafucile. Inside, the Duke and Maddalena are laughing and drinking. Rigoletto is ready to pay for his vengeance.

"Twenty did you say? Here's ten; afterward you'll get the rest."

He will return at midnight to pick up the body. That isn't really necessary; Sparafucile can throw it into the river. But Rigoletto wants to do it himself.

"So be it! What's his name?"

"Would you like to know mine as well?" asks Rigoletto, "His is "Crime'; I am "Punishment.'"

He moves off. The assassin is alone. It is beginning to storm; the night is getting darker. The Duke is not having any luck with the girl. She warns that her brother is coming back. As Sparafucile enters, he mentions that it will soon be raining. Good. The Duke will stay overnight. (The girl whispers that he'd better leave.) In this weather?

Sparafucile is looking forward to earning the rest of his money. He'll be happy to give the Duke a room. As they go upstairs, Maddalena thinks of how gracious that "poor young man" is. "God what a night *this* is!" The pounding music tells us the storm is getting closer. Sparafucile bids his victim good night. The "young man" will soon be asleep; he's tired. He puts his sword near his bed. Before falling off to sleep he starts his flighty, carefree song...but then his voice hesitates and stops.

Again Maddalena comments on how attractive "that young man is." Her brother agrees—twenty crowns worth!

"Only twenty? That's too little—he's worth more."

"The sword, he's asleep, go...bring it here."

Just as Maddalena is handing over the sword to her brother, Gilda shows up on the road dressed as a man with boots and spurs! Her love for the Duke has made her blind to what he really is. (The humming of ghostly voices accent the wind and the rain.)

"My father—forgive me. What a night of horror!"

She looks inside and hears the girl speaking to her brother. She wants him to spare his victim. She thinks the young man is so handsome—like Apollo. She loves him. . .just as he loves her. . .she wants to wait awhile before he's killed! Gilda is trembling.

But Sparafucile throws his sister a sack and orders her to sew it up. That's where he'll put "her Apollo" and then throw him into the river. Gilda believes she's looking into the depths of hell!

Maddalena keeps on trying to convince her brother not to kill the Duke. He can get the whole twenty just by killing Rigoletto instead! Gilda can't believe her ears! Sparafucile is also astonished.

"Kill the hunchback? What the devil are you saying? Do you think I'm a burglar? A bandit? Who of my customers have I ever betrayed? This man pays me, he has my word."

His sister threatens to warn her new love. "Oh—*that's* a good girl!" Doesn't she realize that they'll lose the money? But she keeps insisting that there must be a way to save him. Finally, Sparafucile suggests that if anyone else knocks on the door before midnight, he'll kill him instead. Maddalena doesn't have much faith in that—the night is too bad. Who would be around on a night like this?

In a lively trio, the girl repeats that no one will show up. . .her brother again promises to kill the first one who arrives. . .while Gilda is thinking about sacrificing herself!

"Oh what a temptation! To die for that ungrateful one! To die. . .and my father! Oh Heaven, have pity on me!"

There is still a half hour before midnight. Gilda is surprised to see Maddalena in tears! She knows that there's nothing the girl can do. She, Gilda, because of her love, will give up her life so that he may live.

She knocks on the door. Maddalena hears it. Her brother thinks it's the wind. No...it's someone knocking. That's strange—who could it be?

"Have pity on a beggar...grant him a refuge for the night..."

"It'll be a long night for *him*!" comments Maddalena.

Sparafucile goes for his dagger! Maddalena can't wait for him to stab the stranger! The murderer is ready! All three voice what they want and what they think. Gilda thinks of how close to death she is...she who is so young! She asks forgiveness from her father for giving up her life for the one she loves...she knocks once again.

"Enter...enter..."

"Open..."

"Oh God! Forgive them!" pleads Gilda.

The storm in the heavens matches the storm on earth. Thunder and lightning fill the sky. In seconds Gilda goes through the door...is quickly smothered...and then stabbed! The terrible scene is covered with darkness.

Then as the storm begins to move on...Rigoletto comes into sight. His revenge is about to be satisfied! He has spent thirty days weeping "tears of blood" in the costume of a fool...

What's this? The inn is shut! Well, he'll wait—it isn't midnight yet. What a strange night. A tempest in the skies...and on earth a murder.

There's the sound of a clock striking. Midnight! He knocks on the door.

"Who's there?"

"It's me."

"Wait...here's your dead man!"

"Oh good! Let me have a light!"

But Sparafucile doesn't want *that*. No...just give him the

money—then they'll throw the body in the river. Rigoletto gives him a purse but wants to take care of the rest himself. That's all right with Sparafucile. He advises him to go up the river a ways because it's wider and deeper. Quickly! Before somebody comes! Then in a very deep voice he bids him "Good night..."

Alone now, Rigoletto is overcome with joy! He looks at the sack.

"He's in there! Dead! I want to see him! But what's the difference? He's in there! There are his spurs! Now look at me, world! Here is a fool...and there is a nobleman! He is under my feet! Right there! Oh joy!"

Rigoletto is gloating over his final vengeance. The river will be his enemy's tomb...a sack will be his shroud. To the river! To the river!

Here is where the full force of the drama takes hold. As the hunchback is struggling to drag the sack to the water, he hears a voice in the distance. From his bedchamber the Duke takes up his rollicking song once more! "Women are as flighty as a feather in the wind...!"

The jester stops dead in his tracks. That voice! Can it be a dream? No—it's *him*! The voice dies away. Rigoletto is stupified. Who, then, is in the sack? With trembling hands he opens it up. It *is* a body. Then the weakening storm gives off a flash of lightning. And in that flash he sees the figure of his daughter! His daughter! No...it's impossible! She's on her way to Verona! But then the awful truth comes to him. *She is here!* The sky lights up again.

"Oh my Gilda! Little girl...answer me!"

In his hobbling way he rushes to the inn door. He beats on it. He calls. Silence.

"No one...no one...my daughter...my Gilda...oh my daughter!"

To his surprise he hears a faint cry.

"Who is calling me?"

"She is speaking! She's moving! She's alive! Oh God! Ah, the only one I love on this earth. . . Look at me, recognize me."

Gilda calls to her father. He's puzzled as to what happened. Was she wounded? Yes. . .right there, near her heart. But who was it? The music begins a light melody.

In a weak, painful voice she reveals that she had not done what he wanted; it was her fault. She loved the Duke too much—now she is dying for him! Her father is horrified to think that his daughter actually was a victim of his own revenge.

"Dear angel. . .look at me, listen to me. . . speak to me, dearest daughter!"

Gilda knows that soon she will be forever silent. She wants him to forgive her for what she has done and to forgive the Duke as well. She asks him to bless his dying daughter. . .A gentle, sweeping melody follows her as she tries to comfort him. . .

"In heaven above, near my mother, I shall be for all eternity. . .praying for you. . ."

Joining her in the beautiful strains, Rigoletto begs her not to die. . .not to leave him there alone. . .all alone. Their voices blend thrillingly as the music becomes louder and louder.

But then, at last, with Gilda still promising to pray for him. . .while her father is pleading with her not to leave him there alone. . .there is a final soft refrain, as Gilda dies in his arms. His voice filled with torture and grief, the lonely jester gives an anguished cry.

"Gilda! My Gilda! She's dead! Ah! *The curse!*"

His voice lingers on the last terrible word. The orchestra's drums rumble violently and the cymbals clash as the poor jester falls senseless on the body of his beloved Gilda. The dark, lonely scene closes the dramatic work that has held the stage for over one hundred and thirty years.

THE CURTAIN FALLS

With Rigoletto (although written over ten years before), Verdi matched the force and drive of Wagner's masterpiece *Tristan and Isolde*. The plot is simple and direct; the music spells out each dramatic moment, so the tension builds from start to finish.

In a very real way Gilda also matches Isolde's love for Tristan. Although she begins as an innocent, yet passionate, teenager, we can see her grow up into a woman willing to die for the man she loves. Isolde would have done the same even if Tristan had *not* returned her love.

Although the play was a "scandal" when performed in Paris in 1832, the opera was a huge success on opening night in Venice, in 1851. Everybody was excited about the power of the music and naturally the Verdian melodies—especially the irresistable *cavatina* the Duke sings about "changeable women," and the unsurpassed quartet.

Years later, even Victor Hugo, who hated having his plays made into operas (and who had tried to get the opera banned from France), leaped up to applaud. He later said that he, too, could have had such an impact if he was able to have four people all talk at once and still be understood!

Rigoletto came to New York on February 9, 1855 to the Academy of Music, but had to wait for the first season of the Metropolitan to be performed there on November 16, 1883. (The stars then were the wonderful Marcella Sembrich as Gilda, Roberto Stangno as the Duke and Luigi Guadagnini as Rigoletto). And almost exactly twenty years later, on November 23, 1903, one of the greatest Dukes of all time made his debut in the part—Enrico Caruso.

Today we can visit the small duchy of Mantua and wonder if there might really have been a dashing Duke. Yes. There was a ruling family named Gonzaga in Mantua from 1328 to 1707. Any one of the nineteen dukes that governed during this time could have fit the part. They were all of the same kind of nature, especially a duke known as Vincent I. Among other things, he first married the daughter of the Duke of Parma (nearby) named Margherita Farnese. After the Pope was asked to annul the union, he married the daughter of the Grand Duke of Tuscany, Eleanore de'Medici. Meanwhile, he carried on with "this one and that one" just as Verdi wrote right in the first scene of the first act!

As for the Gonzaga women, there is one fascinating (and amusing) story about the lovely Duchess Giulia. It seems that the feared Turkish pirate Barbarossa (Red Beard) landed with 2000 men and tried to kidnap her and take her back to Constantinople. Instead, she leaped on her horse with nothing on but a smock and escaped, her wonderful head of hair flying in the wind!

Today, you can still see the palace . . . made up of fifteen courtyards and five hundred rooms! Whether there was a court jester like Rigoletto nobody knows. But it's interesting to think, as you look up at the big palace from the ancient central plaza of Mantua called the Piazza Sordella, that there might have been such a court with the kind of people that were made immortal by the genius of Verdi.

The second in the trio of operas that make up the composer's "middle period" has been called by some his most melodious work. But when one thinks of *La Forza Del Destino* or *La Traviata*, then a lot of arguments about that can come up. No question that *Il Trovatore* is one of Verdi's most tuneful operas. In fact, the music is so important, and the characters so well done, that we can almost forget the plot itself. A lot of people would like to do just that because they believe it is too complicated and *un*believable.

Yet, how more mixed up can a story be than the "soap operas" on television? It has to be remembered that centuries ago gypsies were thought of as mysterious people, ones to be feared, and people with such fiery passions that they were able to do almost anything—no matter how "crazy." Today we know better . . . and gypsy or no gypsy, we know that anybody can be so crazed by inside emotions that they are not responsible for what they might do. The gypsy we will soon meet is that kind of a person.

To meet her we must go back to the Spain of the 1400's. It is here that the twenty-three year old Spanish playright, Antonio Garcia Gutierrez, set his play, *El Trovador* in 1836.

Verdi had known of the drama and it interested him. Especially the character of the old gypsy woman. He was so taken with her that at one time he was going to call the opera *Azucena* (her name) or *La Zingera* (*The Gypsy*).

Salvatore Cammarano, his librettist of three earlier operas, was again called upon. He had almost finished the story when he died on July 17, 1852. It was completed by the Neapolitan poet Leone Emmanuele Bardare. Verdi was shocked by the death of his friend; and although they had agreed on a fee of 500 ducats, Verdi paid the poor widow (with children) 600 for the work her husband had already done.

Again, it is a story about young people. Once more, there is a teenager in love who wants to save the boy she loves. And again the plot has to do with *revenge*. This time the vengeful one is the old gypsy who, in her search for revenge, causes something to happen that she never wanted.

And so let us go to the Kingdom of Aragon, in northeast Spain...to the Aliaferia Palace...where the brooding, violent action of *The Troubadour* (The Wandering Minstrel) begins.

5

Il Trovatore

(Eel Troh-Vah-TOH-reh)

ACT I

At the palace of the Count Di Luna (Count of Luna), in Saragossa, we see some guards and manservants. The opening music is a soft rumble of the kettle drums, repeated three times. Then a fanfare...and the sound of a distant trumpet. Violins start a short introduction...as Ferrando, Captain of the Guards, comes in to "stir up" the men sitting around an open fire. (If there is one thing that seems to be there again and again, besides the gypsy's revenge, it is *fire* itself. Fire is everywhere...whether in the heart of Di Luna who loves Leonora...or at the stake where horrible things will happen.)

"Attention!...attention!" orders Ferrando.

He mentions that the Count is deep in thought about his dream of love; keeping guard inside the castle is the way he spends his nights.

The men comment that jealousy is like a snake in his breast. And Ferrando (Feh-RAHN-do) explains that a certain minstrel comes during the night to sing a serenade from the garden. He is a rival whom the Count fears. What is the true story? What happened to shatter his sleep?

"I'll tell you," agrees the Captain. "Gather around me."

The soldiers, too, want to hear. (They all know that something occurred a little over twenty years ago, but they don't really know what.)

Ferrando begins. Two sons had been born to the old Count Di Luna. A faithful nurse of the younger son was sleeping next to the crib. One morning, at the break of dawn, she was awakened by the sun. And what did she find next to that baby?

"Who? Who...who was it?" they all ask anxiously.

To an almost marching beat, Ferrando goes into his aria.

"An old gypsy, with black looks! Strung with symbols of witchcraft! And at the little one...she cast her bloodshot eyes! The nurse was filled with horror...she gave a piercing scream...and in less time than it takes me to tell it, the servants came running into the room. And with threats, shouts, and noise...they chased her back out the way she came!"

All the listeners agree that the servants were right! The wicked witch deserved it! Ferrando goes on.

The gypsy told them that she just wanted to forecast the baby's future. The liar! A low fever slowly took away his health! He was weak and pale, and at night he trembled, while during the day he cried pitifully. She had made him sick!

The Count and his men followed her trail...captured her and condemned her to die by burning at the stake! But that wicked one had left her daughter to carry out her revenge! She stole the little boy and went back to where her mother had died. . .and there we found him. . .*burned to death!*

The men are horrified; they can't imagine such a vile woman. Then they ask about the father, the old Count. His days were short and sad. He had a weird feeling inside that the body they had found was *not* his son's. And he had made the other boy (the present Count) swear that he would never give up the search for his brother!

"Tell us, were you ever able to meet her again?" ask the soldiers.

"Never. Oh, how I wish I could capture her one of these days!"

"But would you be able to recognize her?" wonder the servants.

"Even though the years have gone by—I would."

"Then she could spend the time next to her mother in hell!" suggest the soldiers with satisfaction.

Here Ferrando gives us an understanding of how people in those days thought about witches and gypsies. He believes that on dark nights the lost soul of that dead witch appears to them in different forms! The terrified servants, and even the soldiers, believe that this "is true!" Now their imaginations go wild. In a quick whispering chorus, they talk of how some have seen her on the edge of roofs. She takes many shapes, but especially that of an owl that speeds away with the coming of dawn!

"A servant of the Count died of fright when he suddenly came face to face with the gypsy!" declares Ferrando.

This makes them all even more terrified. . . "he died of fright!" But Ferrando goes right on describing how one night, in the quiet of his room, she showed up as an owl watching with bright eyes. . .making the sky itself clouded with her howling cries! His voice is loud and high.

"And then right at that moment midnight sounded," finishes the Captain, just as a clock actually strikes twelve.

By this time those around him are petrified; they swiftly hurry away as they chorus "Ah! She's wicked, that infernal witch!" The orchestra gives two final chords and the scene ends.

The strings introduce the next scene. It is the garden at night. There is the young girl, Leonora, waiting, waiting. Inez her maid, hurries to her to ask what can be holding her there. It's late; she must come inside. Leonora doesn't seem to hear.

"Still another night without seeing him!"

"You're feeding a dangerous flame!" warns Inez. "How...where did the first spark ignite in you?"

(Here, again, notice the mention of fire.) Leonora goes on to say that she met a knight, at the tournament; he was all in black, even his feather and his shield—an unknown warrior who won every joust. She placed the winner's wreath on his head. Then civil war broke out and she never saw him again. It was like a morning dream, a fleeting image. He was away such a long, long time...but then...

"What happened?"

"Listen!"

Her long note ends. Then the music introduces her story; in one of the opera's many melodious arias, Leonora sings...

"It was a quiet, calm night with a beautiful, serene sky...The full moon's silvery face showed happiness! Suddenly, in that silent hour (her voice glides upward), sweetly and gently came the sound of a harp... and the sad verses a troubadour sang..." (Leonora's voice is now high and thrilling.)

They were words of prayer and humility, like those of a man praying to God. In the midst of them she heard a name...her own name! (Again her voice soars upward.) She knew that her joy in meeting him had been a gift from the angels! In her heart, at his adoring glances, it seemed like heaven on earth! She's ecstatic as she remembers that time, her voice playing over the words in wonderful high *coloratura* expression.

Inez is worried for her mistress. Why? She doesn't quite know, but this unknown man awakens in her a bad omen. Leonora must try to forget him. What? She doesn't want to hear another word! In a quick, almost breathless way, Leonora pours out her feelings for him. Forget him! Inez is talking crazy. No words can destroy her love. Her heart is overcome...her fate can be nothing else but to be near him.

"If I cannot live for him...for him I will die!"

There it is; as her voice ends on a wonderful high note, we hear right at the start her vow of death. With Inez pleading that she should not think of such a love, they go back into the castle and the music comes to a close. The garden is empty, but not for long.

The Count enters; he is hopelessly in love with Leonora. Softly he sings...

"Silent is the night! Deep in sleep...is that royal lady. But her lady-in-waiting is awake... Oh, Leonora...you're there...the flickering light in the window from your night-lamp tells me so. Ah! The flame of love fires all of me!..."

He can't resist any longer. He will go to her...he is looking forward to their "supreme" moment together! He starts for her room and then suddenly stops. Far off he hears the voice of the minstrel!

The troubadour is singing of being alone on earth...of having to go to war—and having only one hope—the hope that a certain heart will be given to him! The Count is fearful.

"...And if that heart...is faithful to him...then richer than any king will be the troubadour," sings the minstrel, hitting a high note.

And so Manrico (Mahn-REE-co)—the romantic black knight—declares his love for Leonora. The Count is burning with jealousy.

He sees Leonora coming from the castle and covers himself with his cape. She mistakes him for her lover!

Hurriedly, she goes to him and calls him her beloved. The Count is puzzled. But she goes on saying how long she has waited until, at last, "merciful love" has guided him into her waiting arms. In the shadows, Manrico, feeling betrayed, calls out "unfaithful one!" Just then, the moon sheds light on a figure with a helmet. The violins play with excitement. Leonara instantly recognizes the voice she has been hoping to hear. She realizes her mistake—the darkness had trapped her. It was to him that her words of love had been spoken. She falls to her knees.

> "I love you, I swear it, I love you...with a great, eternal love!"

Manrico gently raises her; he understands. But the Count is "ablaze with fury." (Notice again the reference to fire.) The young lovers emotionally declare their love for one another. The angry Count demands to know who this man is. Leonora is afraid. Manrico raises his visor.

> "Look at me, I am Manrico!"

> "You! Reckless madman! Follower of Urgel (rebel forces)...condemned to die...what boldness made you turn up at these royal gates?"

Manrico asks him what he is waiting for. Call the guards and have his "rival" fall to the headsman's axe! The Count will do just that. Manrico's "fatal instant" is very close now. Leonora pleads with Di Luna for mercy...to stop!

> "Follow me!" orders the Count. "Let's go!"

Leonora is desperate. What can she do? If she screams, it will only make matters worse. In a long, high note, she begs Di Luna to "listen to her!" The Count is crazy with jealousy. His rage pours out.

> "No!...With jealous love...scorned love...a fearful fire burns in me! His blood...will soon put it out!"

Because Leonora has foolishly declared her love, her lover can no longer live. Di Luna tells her, in a gliding melody, that her very words have condemned Manrico to death! All three voices now blend in a hurried trio:

Leonora asks the Count to think a moment. Since she alone is the reason for "so much fire" in him...then let him take out his fury on her! Let him plunge his sword into her heart...a heart that will not, cannot, love him! Manrico will take care of Di Luna's "vanity and anger" by running him through with his sword! His luck has already run out...his hour has arrived! Fate has ordered that he win Leonora's heart at the same time that he takes Di Luna's life! Throughout, as they repeat their words, the Count continues to threaten to put out "the fire of his love" with Manrico's blood. Then, with Leonora's voice reaching a wonderful high "C," the act comes to a dramatic close.

ACT II

Along the mountains of Biscay lies the gypsy camp. It is almost dawn. Old Azucena (Ah-zoo-CHEH-nah) is sitting by a roaring fire. Manrico is lying nearby covered in his cape. The gypsies are beginning to get ready for the day's work. The orchestra, with pipes screaming, is heard as the voices begin probably *the* best known melody in opera. Before they start to swing their hammers against their anvils, they greet the dawn.

"Look! The night mists are leaving revealing the huge dome of the sky...It looks like a window that has finally shed the blanket in which it was wrapped. To work—strike the hammer!"

The famous "Anvil Chorus" is about to begin. To the steady beat of iron against iron, the gypsies sing their song.

"Who makes a Spanish gypsy's day beautiful...? The Little Gypsy! Pour me out a treat; drinking gives strength and courage to body and soul..."

The women bring wine as the men see a ray of sunlight flashing on the glass! The clanging chorus continues, repeating how beautiful the gypsy women are. They soon gather around Azucena who is staring into the fire. Looking worn and haggard, her eyes thinking of revenge, she begins her driving song.

"Shrieked the blazing flame...!
The crowd...rushes to that fire...
happy to see! Shouts of joy echo all about...
The dark flames rise, rise to the sky!
Shrieked the blazing flame...the victim
is coming...dressed in black, loose and barefoot!
Violent screams calling for death cry out...
echoing from cliff to cliff!
The dark flames rise, rise to the sky!"

Her voice rising with the word, the distracted woman looks sorrowfully at the camp blaze. The trills she sang picture the flickering fire. "How sad her song is," sing the gypsies. But she only repeats that, indeed, the song is sad...because the story is sad. Then out of nowhere she cries the words "Avenge me—avenge me!" Even Manrico is mystified by these strange words that he has heard again and again.

The mood is broken when an old man reminds everyone that the day is getting on. They had better go down to the nearby village if they want to get any bread. "Let's go!" All take up their anvil chorus once more. Their voices get fainter and fainter...as they leave Manrico and his mother alone. The last words heard are "the little gypsy" far away.

Since no one else is around, Manrico wants to know more about the tragic story. Yes, she admits, even he doesn't know it. But then, as a young man he had traveled far and wide. Excited at the memory, she quickly tells of the wicked Count who accused her mother of casting a spell on his son. She was burned at the stake...right there where that fire is now burning! In the aria that follows with its driving rhythm and repeated beat, she continues telling what happened. We hear the shaky strings, the mournful oboe.

"She was lead in chains to her dreadful fate...
With my baby in my arms, I followed her in tears.
I tried, in vain, to find a way to get to her,
In vain I tried to get them to stop, to get her blessing!
But they, with obscene curses, prodded her with swords,
To the stake they tied her...
Then...she cried, 'Avenge me!'
That word echoes always in my heart...
In my heart it remains."

Manrico, awe-struck, asks if she did avenge her. (Here is the part that many people can't believe. But we must remember that the woman had seen the dreadful murder of her mother. She must have been half-crazed with the memory...the roaring fire had destroyed probably the one person that meant the most to her. She must have been blind with anger and misery.)

She describes how she kidnapped the old Count's son...then took him to where the fire was still flaming. Manrico begins to suspect the worst—but he won't be ready for the truth. Again the sight of what happened rises before Azucena's eyes. She sees it all—she hears it all. Her mother screaming for vengeance! Without thinking she reaches down, her eyes staring at the fire...her mind clouded with horror. She feels a small body. In one fast motion she throws it into the flames! (The orchestra sweeps upward.) There's a burst of fire and the victim is gone. Then she gazes around...and right there in front of her is the Count's son! Manrico can't believe his ears! Her voice reaches the heights—"*my son...my son had burned*"

"How horrible...how horrible," gasps Manrico.

"My child...my child!"

Then as she collapses to the ground, her voice low and mournful, she remembers how her hair raised on her head...and still does at the terrible thought.

Now, of course, Manrico wonders who *he* is, if he is not her son. He *is* her son! The gypsy insists he is her son! What does he want from her? After all, when the mind plays tricks...the spirit is clouded...stupid words pass her lips. Hasn't she always been his only mother? He can't deny that. Didn't she save his life when he was wounded in the battle of Pelilla? Manrico remembers his chest wound...how he alone stood against the Count Di Luna. She reminds him of how he had defeated Di Luna—had him under his sword—and did not kill him. Why?

"Oh, mother, I can't even explain it to myself," cries Manrico, holding a long note as he ends.

She wonders at the "strange mercy" that he had shown.

In a swaying melody, Manrico recalls that moment. He had Di Luna at his feet, his sword was raised ready to run him through. Suddenly his hand was stopped by a strange force. His whole body was shaken by a cold shudder! Then a cry came from the sky (a high long note). A cry that told him "do not strike"...His voice ends softly.

Again there's a steady, repeated beat. If he ever has the chance, Azucena wants him to do as she wishes—sink his sword, as far as he can, into Di Luna's heart! Manrico swears that he'll do it!

Just then a horn sounds in the distance. It is a signal from his man, Ruiz. He signals with his own horn. (Azucena hears nothing; she still thinks only of her mother's last words: "Avenge me!") A messenger arrives with a letter. Manrico reads it aloud. They have captured the fort of Castellor and the Prince wants him to take command of its defense. He must hurry. Leonora, believing that he has been killed, is about to enter a convent that very night! Manrico is shocked.

While Azucena asks what is happening, her "son" orders the messenger to go down into the valley and get him a horse. Time is short—fly!

"I'm losing her! Oh, agony! I'm losing that angel!"

Azucena thinks he has lost his mind. She wants him to stay, to listen to her. But he asks her to let him go. She orders him to stay!

> "...Do you want to reopen your chest wound? No, I cannot bear it...your blood is my blood! Every drop that you spill, you are squeezing from my heart!"

Her swinging rhythm is joined by a quick, beautiful tune from Manrico.

> "In a moment my loved one, my hope, could be stolen from me! No...neither heaven nor earth has the power to stop me..."

> "You're mad!" moans Azucena, realizing she has lost.

> "Ah, free my steps...mother—for you'll only have trouble if I stay here; you'll see your son at your feet overcome with grief! Let me go...goodbye!"

And as Manrico's voice rises to cry out his farewell, as his "mother" struggles to hold him back...rich orchestral chords bring the scene to a close.

When the curtains open once more, we find ourselves in the courtyard of the Jerusalem Convent. It is night. Mysterious music is heard along with the plinking of violins. Soon the Count, Ferrando and his men creep in. They are covering themselves with their cloaks.

The Count notes that all is deserted. The hour has not yet arrived when the nuns sing the services. He is on time! Ferrando warns him that he is taking a great risk.

> "A risk that my mad love and damaged pride demand!"

Now that his rival is dead, it seemed that nothing stood in his way—and then Leonora calls on a new and more powerful force—the altar!

No! The altar will not claim Leonora—"Leonora is mine!" He holds onto the last word. Then gently, romantically, he leads into one of the opera's loveliest baritone arias. For a moment we see that Di Luna is only human after all—a man hopelessly in love.

"The flash of her smile captures the ray of a star! The brightness of her beautiful face fills me with new courage. Ah...love...burning love speaks in my favor! The sunshine of her glance calms the storm of my heart..."

The music has stopped as he sings the last two lines...then softly comes back in to accompany him to a close.

The chapel bell sounds! It is time! Before Leonora reaches the altar, he will kidnap her! The Count orders his men to leave... to hide in the shadows of the trees. He gloats over the fact that soon she will be his...he is "filled with a fire" of expectation.

Whispering, Ferrando and the others speak of leaving, hiding, being quiet so that the Count will get his wish. A horn fanfare introduces a lively *cabaletta*. The Count sings of his final victory.

"For me, fatal hour, your moments are speeding along... there are no words for the kind of joy that awaits me! In vain does a rival God oppose this love of mine!" (His voice soars.)
"No, no, even God Himself, my lady, cannot take you from me!"

Again the soldiers sing their "hiding song"...as the Count himself joins them under the trees.

In a chorus of soft, heavenly voices, the nuns inside are telling the "daughter of Eve" (Leonora) that life on earth is but a shadowy dream. She is to wear a veil that will hide her from all eyes. She is to forget all earthly thoughts...turn to Heaven...and Heaven will welcome her.

Leonora comes in with her friend Inez who is crying at the thought that her mistress is about to leave her forever. In a sweet lyric strain Leonora explains that "a smile, a hope, a flower on earth" is not for her. Perhaps one day she will again be united with her loved one who "is lost." She no sooner starts toward the altar than the Count steps out!

"No, never!"

To the shocked women, he must seem like a ghost. Leonora can't believe that he had the nerve to come to the convent...a sacred place. He is there to claim her as his own. Before another move, Manrico appears! Leonora can't believe this either. Manrico alive...standing there before her! The strings start a quick, light beat. Her voice climbs...perhaps it's all a dream. Her heart is rapidly throbbing with joy.

"Have you come down from heaven... or am I in heaven with you?"

Now follows a marvelous blending of voices...repeated rhythms...excited violins. The Count and Manrico talk about his "return from the dead." He has returned either from heaven or hell. The Count's hateful men had, indeed, given him a mortal wound. Well, since it didn't work the first time, the Count declares that now his days are really numbered. Manrico threatens him in return..."God is on my side!" Di Luna will let him live...but he must "fly from her, and from me."

Meanwhile, Leonora repeats her wondering as to whether it is a dream, a fantasy, a superhuman spell! Inez and the nuns comment that because Manrico had faith in God, God took pity on him.

Ferrando and his men, however, see that Manrico has brought his own soldiers, and they warn the Count. But it's too late. Ruiz's and Manrico's "brave warriors" take charge. Di Luna tries to resist, but it's no use. In a moment he's disarmed. Ferrando wants his orders, but the Count has lost all sense of reason. Leonora is terrified. The other women are praying that Heaven will have pity.

While Ruiz and his men start to leave—after the Count is driven back and his men have given up—Manrico joins Leonora in song as he takes her away. And to the rumble of drums, the curtain swiftly falls.

ACT III

There's a bright military introduction, then hurried violins, as the scene shows the camp of Count Di Luna. They are trying to get back the captured fort of Castellor. Soldiers are everywhere...some looking after their equipment, others gambling. They start off a rollicking soldier's chorus.

"Pretty soon we'll be playing a different kind of game...These swords...bright with blood...with blood will soon be stained!"

A band of men with cross-bows enter the camp. It's the help they ordered! The attack on Castellor will soon begin. Ferrando agrees. The next morning the attack will start...and they will get more booty than they've ever dreamed! Then, swinging into a tuneful rhythm, Ferrando and the soldiers sing of how the "horns of war" will blare and echo...calling them to the attack. They think of how victory will smile on them!

"There wealth and glory waits for us...There will be the greatest plunder and honor!"

And the soldiers march off, singing of the victory they will have the next day!

The stage is now empty as the Count comes out of his tent and looks at the fort where the woman he loves is in his rival's arms. The thought is driving him crazy.

"In the arms of my rival!...but I'm hurrying...as soon as dawn breaks...I'll run to separate them! Oh, Leonora," he sings sadly.

Before he can go on, Ferrando rushes in. Near the camp a gypsy was seen circling around; she tried to escape when she was surprised by the scouts. But she was captured. And here she is!

In a moment, soldiers drag in the tied up Azucena. She's struggling to get free as she demands to know what harm she has done.

"Come here. Answer my questions—and beware of lying!"

"Ask."

"Where were you going?"

"I don't know."

"What?"

"It's the way of a gypsy to wander without direction...
the sky is his roof, the whole world his country."

The questioning goes on. When she tells them that she's from
Biscay, Ferrando begins to suspect who she really is! Azucena
sings sadly of her search for her son. The melody is another
Verdi gem as she repeats that there is no greater love than a
mother's love. Her voice climbs gently as the violins carry the
beautiful aria to a close. Again Ferrando thinks he knows that
face!

Since she has been in these mountains for many years, the
Count wonders if she remembers a child that was stolen from
his castle long ago. Azucena starts to realize who this nobleman
is. He is the brother of the kidnapped baby! The gypsy is terrified! That is all that Ferrando needs to convince him that he's
right.

"Have you ever heard this story?" asks the Count.

"Who me? No!" She wants to leave...to continue her
search.

But Ferrando is sure that she is the one who committed that
horrible crime! The Count wants to know more. "It's her!" cries
Ferrando, as the gypsy softly begs him to be quiet.

"She's the one who took the baby!"

"He lies!"

"You shall not escape your fate!...Tie the knots tighter!"

"Oh, God! Oh, God!" cries Azucena, as the Count makes
fun of her screams.

She despairs that Manrico does not come to help her. Why

has her son not come to rescue his mother! As soon as Di Luna hears this, he knows that he has Manrico in his power!

Beginning on a long, high note, Azucena goes into a stirring *cabaletta*, a foot-tapping rhythm. She wants them to let her go...to be free from torture and drawn-out death! She calls out that from a wicked father has sprung a worse son! God will punish him!

To a brisk horn accompaniment, the Count gloats on how he will get his revenge on "that seducer" by torturing his mother. He will be filled with joy...as soon as he has received his revenge. Ferrando and the soldiers join in. They, too, are looking forward to the burning at the stake of this hateful gypsy...who will not only suffer the fire of the stake, but will be damned to the fires of hell forevermore! The voices and orchestra end in a wonderful climax of sound. And at a signal from Di Luna, the soldiers drag Azucena away. The scene comes to a close as the Count goes back to his tent followed by the loyal Ferrando.

In the second scene of the act, we find ourselves in a room of Castellor. The lovers are together. Leonora is alarmed at the sounds of war that she hears. Manrico must admit that they are in great danger. At the break of dawn they will be attacked! In a strong dramatic tenor voice, he assures her that they will be victorious over their enemies. He orders Ruiz to be sure that all is ready for battle.

Leonora soulfully sings of how a gloomy light is cast over their marriage plans. Manrico lovingly bids her to forget her unhappy thoughts. She should think only of love...wonderful love that comes from the heart. His voice is high and soft. Then, to a sweet introduction of the woodwinds, Manrico sings one of the major arias of the opera.

> "Ah! Yes, my love, when I am yours and you are mine...
> my soul will be more fearless, my arm will be more strong.
> And yet, if in the pages of my future it is written that I shall
> be among the victims...that I shall be wounded by a hostile

sword and breathing my last breath...my thoughts will be of you.''

The music falls silent.

''Only if I will see you again in heaven (glorious high note), will death for me seem worthwhile!''

The sound of the organ is heard coming from the chapel. The lovers' hearts are full of their ''pure love'' as they think of being united in marriage. But their dreaming is quickly shattered. Ruiz comes in and excitedly reports that the gypsy has been captured and is in the hands of those barbarians who have already tied her to the stake! The orchestra crashes. Manrico is shaking with fear and anger. Leonora has never seen him this way. Why? What is it? That woman...''I am her son!'' Another crash. Then in quick bursts, Manrico orders Ruiz to gather up the men, to hurry! There are the violins—the power of the full orchestra. To a strong military beat, Manrico flies into a thrilling stormy aria!

''From that pyre! From that horrendous fire...my whole being is inflamed! Godless ones...put it out...or soon I'll put it out with your own blood!...unhappy mother, I'm running to save you...or with you, at least, I shall run to my death!''

His voice reaches the heights as he sings ''with you''...and lingers long over the word ''death.''

In hurries Ruiz and his men. Horns ring out the call to arms! Over and over they call for battle...with Manrico's voice closing on a high ''C'' as it rises above all the others! He rushes out as they all follow him to the fight. A clash of arms is heard as the curtain falls.

ACT IV

It is the palace of Aliaferia. The night is black. Dimly a tower can be seen; its windows are heavily barred. We hear mournful bassoons and other woodwinds, creeping music. Two figures enter wrapped in cloaks. Leonora with Ruiz! He points out the tower where Manrico is being held prisoner. Leonora asks him to leave . . . not to be afraid for her. She may be able to save her lover. When Ruiz is gone, Leonora looks at the ring on her finger.

The violins begin a quivering, threatening sound. A most beautiful aria is about to start.

"Afraid for me? Surely . . . here is my defense! In this dark night . . . I am close to you, and you do not know it! A mournful, gentle breeze, that swirls around, alas, carries my unhappy sighs!"

Her voice is now lyrical, coloratura.

"From love . . . on rosy wings . . . rise painful sighs . . . to comfort the suffering mind of that poor prisoner . . . Like a breath of hope they come to rest in that room! They awaken in him memories, of dreams . . . dreams of love."

The music now expands as her voice climbs gloriously.

"But, alas! They don't tell him . . . of the pain, the pain, the pain . . . in my heart!"

Her voice quivers in a long "trill" on the word "pain" . . . and rises in wondrous *coloratura* as she sings "in my heart" . . . the high violins end this passionate song.

Suddenly there are bells. The voices of monks are heard. It is the start of the famous "Miserere" . . . a steady, mournful rhythm that tells us that Manrico is indeed condemned to death. The monks are praying for his soul . . . to spare it from "eternal flames."

There's a deep, heavy beat as we hear Leonora mention the sound of the bells, the prayers of the monks. The solemn funeral procession fills her with terror . . . leaving her almost breathless, her heart beating rapidly. Then, from the tower, Manrico sings a despairing song . . . as the harp (the traditional minstrels' instrument) accompanies him.

"Ah! How this death that is to come at any hour . . . is so

late in coming... to one who wishes to die! Good-bye, good-bye... Leonora, good-bye!''

Leonora hears him in desperation. The monks' voices continue their sad refrain. Will that horrid tower release her beloved only when he is dead? Manrico reflects that only with his blood will he pay for loving Leonora. Then in a pleading voice he calls out.

"Don't forget me!
Leonora, good-bye!
Leonora, good-bye, good-bye!''

How could she ever forget him? Leonora reaches a high, tragic note as the orchestra swells to a final climax. She sadly leaves. She has hardly disappeared when in strides the Count with some of his men. He is ordering them to execute Manrico and his mother at dawn. Manrico by the headsman's axe, the gypsy by burning at the stake!

Di Luna is now alone. He has some doubts as to whether he was given the power by the Prince to do what he's doing. Then his thoughts turn to Leonora. Even though he had captured Castellor, she was not to be found. They searched and searched, but to no avail. Finally, with bitter grief he sings out.

"Oh! Where are you... cruel one!''

"Right behind you,'' answers Leonora, coming from the darkness.

The Count is amazed! That voice! Could it really be her? Yes. She has come to ask for the life of Manrico. She wants him to have mercy! Mercy! They sweep into a short duet.

"You want me to have pity on my rival?''

"May a merciful God inspire you!''

"Only revenge is my god. Go!'' And Di Luna repeats his vow. Leonora falls to her knees to beg him.

"Look... my bitter tears are flowing around your feet; are my tears not enough? Then slay me... spill my blood, trample on my body...but save the troubador!''

But Di Luna is blind with rage. He would rather increase Manrico's torture a thousand times...have him die a hundred deaths! The more she loves Manrico...the more terrible are the flames that drive Di Luna's fury! Here, then, Leonora is forced to play her last card. She clings to the Count as he starts to go. She begs him for pity, but he wants her to leave him. She has one last thing to give him—and she is offering it now.

"Explain yourself...what price...tell me?''

"Myself!''

"God! What did you say?'' (The violins enter.)

"And you know that I will keep my promise.''

"Am I dreaming?''

She wants him to just open the prison gates and let Manrico go—and she will be his. She swears it! At this the Count calls to a jailor.

While he whispers his orders we see Leonora take the poison that is in her ring! All that Di Luna will have of her is a cold and lifeless body! As soon as Di Luna announces that the prisoner will live, Leonora in a light, quick *coloratura* happily sings of her joy at the news.

"He will live! Happily and joyfully!''

The Count joins her in the lively duet. He wants only to have her say that she is his...to repeat that she is his...so that he can finally believe her!

"Let's go. Sacred is my word,'' answers Leonora, ending in a thrilling high "C''!

"You have sworn—remember!'' cries the Count, as they both leave for the tower. The scene closes.

The next, and final, scene takes place in a filthy dungeon. Deep strings play in a monotone; others come in for the long introduction. Azucena lies on a straw bed, Manrico beside her.

"Mother, aren't you sleeping?"

"I've tried many times...but sleep flies from my eyes! I'm praying."

Manrico wonders whether the cold air is making her shiver. But it is only the "tomb" from which she would like to escape; her very breath is being suffocated. She asks him not to be saddened about her; the cruel ones will not put her to torture. Why? Because you can tell by just looking at her face that she will soon die! They will only find a dead, cold body—perhaps even a skeleton. Manrico doesn't want to hear any more. Shaking violins follow her next words. Doesn't he hear them—getting closer? The executioners are coming to drag her to the flaming pyre. He must defend his mother!

Manrico tries to comfort her, but she can only repeat over and over..."the pyre, the pyre, the pyre...what a horrible word!" Once again she remembers that far-off day when her mother was taken in chains to the roaring flames. Her burning hair sending sparks into the sky! Her eyes staring from their sockets! Her voice rises as she wishes that this frightful memory could be taken from her.

Manrico tries to comfort her. Tenderly he tells her that if she still loves him...she will forget and rest and stay calm. To the deep plinking of the strings, they begin a melodious duet. Yes, she is really tired...she will try to close her eyes. But she still fears the fire, the horrid flames! Manrico's voice tries to calm her.

"Rest, Oh mother! God will take the sadness from your heart."

The steady, soft strings beat to her words as she begins an unhappy refrain.

"To our mountains we shall return and the old peace in that place we will enjoy! You will sing, and play on your lute... While I sleep a tranquil sleep."

Manrico again bids her to rest...while the dying Azucena repeats her hopeful words once more.

In the next moment, the door opens and Leonora hurries in. Manrico can't believe his eyes. Is it really Leonora? Has God allowed him one last joy before he is to die? The music hurries along with Leonora's answer. He is not to die—she has come to save him! Quickly, quickly...He must leave at once! Isn't she coming? She will remain! Manrico refuses to go. He begins to suspect the worst. His life is nothing to him. Silence.

> "Look me in the eyes! What bargain have you made—and at what price? You do not want to speak? ...Ha...you sold our love—you sold a heart that you swore was mine!"

> "Oh, how wrong you are! Oh, how your anger has blinded you!"

But Manrico will not understand. She has betrayed their love. Still, Leonora begs him to flee before it is too late—"when even God will not be able to save him!" And while the poor girl tries to convince her love to save himself...we hear the old gypsy sing of her home in the mountains.

In a last desperate try, Leonora falls at Manrico's feet. He wants her to get away—he has come to hate her, to curse her! He doesn't know the sacrifice she has made—to give up her life for his. She pleads with him to stop cursing her; instead she needs his prayers to God...in this hour. Calling his name, she falls to the stones of the cell.

At last he sees that something is very wrong. He hastens to her and raises her as she tells him that death is in her breast. Death! Yes, the force of the poison was quicker than she had thought!

> "Listen! My hand is cold...but here (in her breast) there is a terrible fire!"

> "What have you done—oh, God!" cries Manrico.

Slowly her voice climbs as she looks at him. She would rather have died as his own than live belonging to another. (Remember Isolde?) Manrico realizes what a great love "this angel" has for him—a love he had just recently cursed.

". . . I am dying, Manrico," she whispers as she clasps his hand.

And there is the Count Di Luna! He sees at once that Leonora has tried to trick him. Again she sings, in a heavenly voice, that she would rather have died than belong to another. Manrico can't believe that he had really doubted her love. Calling his name for the last time, Leonora, in a long, high note, sings "goodbye, I die!". . . as the violins play sweetly and the orchestra thunders a final chord. Although he calls her name, it is too late.

Now, in rapid order. . . the last words of the story are spoken.

"Take him to his execution!" (Crash of the music!)

"Mother—Oh, my mother!" (Crash!)

"Manrico—where is my son?" (Crash!)

"To his death he runs!" calls DiLuna.

"Ah, stop! Listen to me!" (Crash!)

Di Luna drags Azucena to the window.

"Look at him!"

"Heavens!" (Crash!)

"He's dead!"

"*He was your brother!*" (The orchestra quivers.)

"Eh! How horrible!" cries the Count in anguish.

"You have your vengeance, Oh mother!" calls Azucena, as she collapses at the window.

Horrified at what he has done, Di Luna can think of only one thing to say: "And *I* still live!". . . while the music ends in repeated chords. . .

THE CURTAIN FALLS

And so the blood and thunder of this great dramatic story comes to a close. Again, as with *Rigoletto*, we see a revenge that misfires—a loving "mother" who brings about the death of the one person she truly loves. Through his music and the vivid people he created, Verdi was able to minimize the plot. Just as in Wagner's *Tristan and Isolde*, we take away with us the memory of this great love. We forget the potion; we forget the mistake of the child being thrown into the flames. We have been fully taken into the lives and the torment of the powerful characters Verdi's music and his writers have created.

Il Trovatore was first performed at the Apollo Theatre in Rome on January 19, 1853. As has happened many times since, the Tiber River that flows through the city flooded and the audience had a lively time trying to get into the lobby. But the wet shoes and feet must have been worth it. The opera received such an ovation that the cast was not allowed to leave until the end of the third act and the entire fourth act were performed over again!

On May 2, 1855, *Il Trovatore* was performed for the first time in America at the New York Academy of Music. But it had to wait for the Metropolitan Opera House to open its doors before it played there on October 25, 1883. Giuseppe Verdi lived to the age of eighty-seven and had composed twenty-six operas in all. *Trovatore* was his seventeenth opera—a master work written in only twenty-eight days. He had become a rich man and devoted a great amount of time to his Villa—the farm of Sant'Agata. Strangely, from the time of the debut of *Aida* on Christmas Eve 1871 until the premiere of *Otello*, February 5, 1887, he wrote no opera. In the meantime, he lived unmarried for twelve years with Giuseppina Strepponi (who had been a leading singer) and who, before and after their marriage in 1859, was his steady companion for fifty years.

It was his love of William Shakespeare, and the wonderful writing of Arrigo Boito, that brought him out of retirement and resulted in what many believe are his greatest works—*Otello* and *Falstaff*. Critics of the time believed the old man's powers had left him, but as one of them wrote after *Otello*, it took only the sound of that first tremendous chord to know once and for all that Verdi was back!

But finally, on January 21, 1901, the great composer, the man who did as much with his music to liberate Italy as any man with a gun, suffered a paralyzing stroke. He seemed to fall asleep, breathing steadily until the morning of January 27... when at last the end came.

Since he was a simple man, a man who wrote of basic human emotions, it is not surprising that he left in his will a request that his funeral be "very modest, either at dawn or the time of the Ave Maria in the evening, and without music and singing." He also wanted to be buried beside his Giuseppina. And so early in the morning, with only a few friends near him, he was carried in an ordinary hearse to be buried as he wished.

But then a wonderful sound began, a sound that could not be kept inside. Softly, from the throats of the sorrowing few, came the words and melody of his great chorus from *Nabucco*.

"Go, thought, on golden wings...
Go, rest yourself on the slopes and hills...
Where, soft and warm, murmur
the sweet breezes of our native soil."

It was not to end there. Verdi had also asked that he and his wife be buried in the home he had created for elderly musicians— the Casa di Riposo, the House of Rest. So on February 28, the two coffins were removed from the cemetery to start their last journey. But this time it was very different!

Under the leadership of Arturo Toscanini, a chorus of eight hundred voices began the "Va, pensiero." All of Milan, it seemed, stood along the way and joined the chorus in their last tribute to the man who wrote so passionately about the human heart. And in bidding him goodbye, they seemed to remember the words of the great poet, D'Annunzio, who memorialized him by saying, "He wept and loved for all."

And so once again we leave Spain and Italy in our travels, and through music we move along to a different continent. This time we are looking forward to visiting an ancient land...where white-robed figures roam on lurching camels...desert sands blow and form an almost endless wasteland. In the distance we may see a palm-fringed oasis and even further along the dim shapes of pyramids. We are going to the north of Africa to the mystic country of Egypt—bounded on one side by the blue Mediterranean and on another by the Red Sea.

Who will be our guide this time? A young man, short and thin, with a head a bit too large for his small body but topped by a flowing wealth of hair. His name is Wolfgang Amadeus Mozart (WOLF-gang Ah-mah-DAY-us MOTE-zahrt)...one of the towering geniuses of all time.

To meet him properly, we should go back to the Salzburg, Austria of January 27, 1756. On that day was born a master who to this day stands alone—one who poured out music unique in its purity, clarity and perfection.

At three years he began showing amazing interest in the early keyboard instrument known as a claviar. At four, his father began teaching him how to play. It is known that he had such a fine ear that he could catch a violin that was tuned even an eighth of a note off! He could play a variety of melodies on a single theme—without repeating himself—for half an hour. He could read music instantly and play it perfectly without practice.

One day he was found writing a concerto, full of blots of ink. His father and a favorite musician friend looked it over. Finally, his father turned to his friend (Schachtner) and in an unbelieving voice, noted that the child had not only written a concerto, but one that was too difficult for anyone to play.

A favorite story describes the time that a usual gathering of music makers was about to start on a new set of six trios at father Mozart's house. Little Wolfgang insisted on playing second violin. His father objected, but kindly Schachtner changed his mind. Especially on hearing the tot cry out: "Papa, surely you don't have to study...to play *second* violin, do you?" Upon which, in the company of the others, the five year old played all of the pieces perfectly!

And so it went: a complete sonata at seven, a symphony at eight. By this time his father, Leopold, had taken him over most of Europe where the child prodigy amazed all, including kings and queens, as well as legendary musicians such as Joseph Haydn.

But strangely enough, his time of glory was running out. Can you imagine being a "has-been" by the age of eleven? Oh, not that Mozart's talent had worn away—he was yet to produce his greatest works. But simply that a boy of eleven was not as great a marvel as a child of five! Luckily, his father was the kind of man who pushed and shoved and promoted. Through him the genius of his son was not allowed to die. And so, along with his sister who was only a few years older, the team continued to play and amaze—but not as before.

All through his life the jealousy of others in the music world was the major reason for his lack of financial success. *Mozart never made a lot of money from his music!*

With his sister Marianne, affectionately called Nannerl, Wolfgang (Wolferl) spent twelve years "on the road." Any money that was earned usually went for keeping up the "appearances" of this little troupe. Finally, when in Vienna, the Emperor himself had to use his power to get young Mozart an order for an opera. The result was *La Finta Semplice* which the narrow-minded people of the opera house made sure was never performed! Only in the house of a famous hypnotist, Dr. Franz Anton Mesmer (whose name has come down to us in the word "mesmerize"), was a little opera called *Bastien und Bastienne* presented. (Although it is never heard today, we can still hear some notes borrowed by Beethoven for the opening of his *Eroica* Symphony!)

Fortunately, Leopold had always dreamed of going to Italy, and so they did. At that time Naples was the center of the opera world. There, at fourteen, he was hailed as the great musician he really was. But it was in Rome that he astounded everyone.

During Holy Week, every year from the time it was written

by Gregorio Allegri around the end of the sixteenth century, a *Miserere* was sung by the Pope's choir. It was strictly forbidden—under the threat of being banned from the church—for anyone to write it down or even hum it a little anywhere. Well, Wolfgang and his father went to hear the performance. Just once.

When he came back to his room, Mozart began writing the whole thing *from memory*! By morning it was complete. Of course, the Pope soon found out about this unbelievable achievement. He was so overwhelmed, that instead of punishing the boy, he awarded him the Cross of the Order of the Golden Spur! But these glory days were short-lived.

Back in Vienna, he was blocked in every way possible. But the fire inside him was never put out. In spite of Antonio Salieri, the court's favorite musician, the people loved Mozart's opera, *The Abduction from the Seraglio*. Concerto followed concerto; symphony after symphony poured out. *The Marriage of Figaro* (remember *The Barber?*) was finished in six weeks.

Yet all along, Mozart met with jealousy...all along he led a poor man's life. To add to his troubles, his body had been weakened by early sicknesses. Even his native Austrian fun-loving spirit was not enough to deal with his unhappy life. At last, when there seemed no hope left at all, an actor and im-pressario by the name of Emanuel Schikaneder called on him to write a German opera. And so his master-work was born—*Die Zauberflöte...The Magic Flute*.

How wonderful this request must have seemed to Mozart. How it must have proved to him that fate was on his side, for he believed with his whole heart in "the force of destiny." He strongly believed that God was the final judge of how fate would treat him. If destiny, through God, wanted it that way, then that's the way it must be!

Mozart went to work. It was July, 1791. By September the opera was finished. Would it be a success? Would the people know what he was trying to say? It must have been with some fear that Mozart watched his opera come to life on the night of September 30, 1791, in Schikaneder's own small theatre named Auf der Wieden. The opera that was to be called his greatest. . .

6

Die Zauberflöte

(Dee Zow-behr-float-eh)

Remember when we talked about *Il Trovatore* we said that many people, including respected critics, think that the plot is not just unbelievable, but much too confusing? Well, when it comes to *that*, no work has received more criticism than *The Magic Flute*.

Some think that Mozart was taking a swipe at the Empress Maria Teresa because she was against Freemasonry—the Masons—a group that has very high moral standards. (Both Mozart and Schikaneder were Masons.) The triumph of good over evil is found in the opera just as it is in the teachings of the Masons.

Whether that's true or not, we'll find that *The Magic Flute* is a comic opera as well as a serious one. It has a lot of spoken words as well as singing just like the old German *Singspiel*. The combination of folk music along with classical music is simply brilliant. And one of the main reasons that it seems a bit confusing is that Mozart had to change all the characters around because another opera came out before his that used the same story! So he changed good to evil and villains to heroes. With that, let's sit ourselves down and enjoy Mozart's last wonderful work. It takes us to far-off Egypt, the Temple of Isis, around the time of the Pharoah Ramses I.

ACT I

The overture opens with three grand chords. Then there is some solemn music followed by lively, happy music. After this there are three fanfares...and again spritely music featuring thin violins. It ends with another three chords.

The curtain rises on a rocky scene, with trees and mountains. There is mysterious yet excited music that introduces our hero, Tamino (Tah-ME-no), who is scrambling to get away from a large snake. He has a bow but no arrows! In a short aria, as he tries to escape, he calls for help..."help me or I am gone!" The snake will certainly eat him if the gods don't come to help him. He falls down in a dead faint. Sure enough, three veiled ladies suddenly appear and with their silver spears kill the serpent.

"Triumph! Triumph! The heroic deed is done! He is free thanks to our brave arms!"

Now they are attracted to the unconscious Tamino. The first one notes that he's "a lovely youngster, gentle and handsome!" The second one thinks that she has never seen one so beautiful. The third agrees that he's as pretty as a picture! Then all three, in a light, comic way say that if ever they should lose their hearts in love...it certainly would be to this young man. But now they have to tell their "Queen of the Night" about him...and perhaps this handsome man can bring back the peace she has lost.

To a steady beat, each one wants the other to go and bring that message. And each one wants to stay with this handsome young man.

"No, no! You can't do that! *I'll* watch over him!"

Well, they're not getting very far. Each keeps insisting, until finally all three sing (to themselves) that they can't agree about leaving any one of them alone with this good-looking lad. They wistfully think of how they would give anything to be able to live with him. . .and have him "for me alone!" But since it doesn't look like that's going to happen, each one decides that she had better go. So, in another light trio, they sing their goodbyes to this "youth, so handsome and so lovable". . .and hope that they'll see him once again, and off they go.

Tamino wakes up in a daze. He doesn't know where he is. Is he dreaming that he is still alive? Or did a "higher power" save him? There's the snake dead at his feet! Suddenly, he hears the sound of piping. What can it be? Who can it be? Tamino quickly hides.

The orchestra plays an introduction as we see a strange figure swinging along. The feathers that are all over him make him look like a bird-man! In fact he has a cage on his back with some birds in it! To a cheery tune, mixed in with playing on his pipes, Papageno (Pa-pa-GANE-oh) tells us all about himself.

"The bird-catcher am I. . .proud to say that as bird-catcher I'm known throughout the land by old and young."

He's very smart at catching birds. . .since they all know his joyful piping. So he's happy and merry. . .because all the birds are his alone!

"The bird-catcher am I. . .always happy, tra-la. . . And yet I'd love to catch a maid. . .to trap them by the dozen! I'd lock them up in my house and all the girls would then be mine!
If all the girls were mine. . .I'd exchange them for some sugar, and all the sugar that I'd get I would give to the one

I like best.

She then would hug me tenderly...she would be my wife just as I would be her husband. She would sleep by my side and I would kiss her as a child."

Now follows a spoken conversation between Tamino and Papageno. (As we said, these unsung parts are what make the work seem like a *Singspiel*).

"Hey there!" calls Tamino.

"Who's there?"

"Tell me, my happy friend, who are you?"

"Who am I? Dumb question! A *man* like yourself. Suppose I ask you who *you* are?"

Tamino explains that his father is a ruler over many countries and people...and that's why "they call me a Prince."

Well, this is quite some news for Papageno. To think that there are other countries, other people. And here's a Prince, too! What this means for his bird-catching! Tamino, in turn, asks about *this* country's name...and "who is its ruler?"

Papageno can answer that just about as much as he can tell him how he came into this world. All he knows is that nearby is his little straw hut that keeps him out of the cold and rain. How does he live? By eating and drinking, like any other man.

Even though it's like pulling teeth, Tamino keeps on trying to find out more about this strange creature. How does Papageno get this food and drink? By catching birds for his "radiant Queen" and her ladies.

Tamino is startled by the mention of a queen. He wonders to himself if it could be the Queen of the Night!

"Tell me, my friend, have you ever had the chance to see her?"

Papageno is aghast! See the radiant Queen? If Tamino has any more idiotic questions like that, as sure as he's called Papageno, he'll lock him up in his cage like a bullfinch and sell him...as he does his other birds...and they can either roast or fry him. What ordinary man has ever seen the Queen? Then he notices that the Prince is staring at him as if he were a freak. Tamino doesn't think that he's a man at all...more like a bird!

"A bird? Listen, you'd better not get too close because I have the strength of a giant," boasts Papageno.

"Were you the one who saved me...the one who killed the poisonous snake?"

At this, Papageno jumps. Snake? What snake? If so, Tamino wants to know, how did he do it without a weapon? Oh, well, Papageno has hands stronger than any weapon. In fact, he just strangled it!

Now he's in trouble. The Three Ladies call out his name. The Prince wants to know who they are...and are they good-looking?

Papageno doesn't really know. All he knows is that they take his birds and he gets food and drink in exchange. As for being beautiful—if they were, they wouldn't go around with their faces covered up! He's just getting himself into more trouble. Now he's done it! The ladies go into action.

Instead of wine, he's getting water. Instead of sweet bread, a stone...and instead of figs—a gold padlock for his mouth! Would he like to know why the Queen is treating him like this? So that he will never again lie to strangers!

All that poor Papageno can do now is mumble "Hm." The Three Ladies then let Tamino know that it was they who saved him...that he should not be afraid, and that joy and pleasure are in store for him. That is, if he likes the picture of this girl who is the daughter of the Queen. If so...all honor, fame and fortune will be his! They start to leave.

"Until we meet again," cry all three.

"Good-bye Sir Papageno!" cries Lady Two.

"Don't drink too fast," teases Lady One.

Tamino and the close-mouthed Papageno are alone once more.

The Prince has already fallen madly in love with the girl in the picture. He sings a flowing aria.

"This picture is bewitching...more than my eye has ever seen! I feel how much this heavenly face has filled my heart with new emotion."

He can't explain this sensation, but he feels it burning in his heart. Could it be love? Of course! It can't be anything else! Oh, if he only knew where she was...if she could already be near him. What would he do? The music stops as he thinks. Then he knows! He would surround her with tenderness...press her to his bosom—and she would be his forevermore!

"She would be mine forevermore," repeats Tamino, as he reaches a high note at the end.

Once again, The Three Ladies appear! This is what they wanted to hear. They speak to him in turn. He has been heard by the Queen and his future is clear. But he must have courage and a strong will. If he really has as much courage as he has tenderness...then Pamina (Pa-ME-nah) is saved!

Tamino is puzzled. Saved? Pamina? And so the ladies explain that the daughter of the Queen of the Night was kidnapped by an evil spirit. His name is Sarastro (Sah-RAH-stroh)! He lives very close to our mountains...in a wonderful castle that's heavily guarded.

"All right, ladies, lead me to it! Pamina will be saved!" declares Tamino. "Good God, what's that?" he cries, as a clap of thunder echoes.

The Three Ladies soon let him know.

"The Queen! She comes! She comes! She comes!"

As they say this, the mountains draw apart! And there she is. After a musical introduction, the lovely Queen assures the frightened Tamino that he has nothing to fear from her. Since he is a young man who is pure, wise and innocent...he may be just the one to comfort a mother's heart that is deeply troubled. Her aria goes on.

"I am fated to suffer, because my daughter was taken from me...All my happiness has gone with her... A scoundrel kidnapped her from me," she cries, holding long on the word "scoundrel."

She can still see her child trembling in fear...shrinking from this evil. "Ah, help!" was all that she could say. But it was no use...since "my help was too weak," sings the Queen with a lyrical *coloratura* voice.

"You will go to free her... You will be the saviour of my daughter!"

(Her coloratura continues beautifully.)

"And if I see you return victorious...she will be yours forever!"

Her voice reaches a high note, then softly ends. And before Tamino can say one word, the mountains come together again and the Queen is gone!

Tamino can't believe what he saw. Comically, Papageno goes to him but can only hum, hum, hum, because of the lock on his mouth. And while he hums along, Tamino tells him how sorry he is that he does not have the power to set him free. In a moment, however, Lady One comes forth to explain that the Queen has taken pity, and he is to be freed of his lock. She instantly takes it away. Papageno once again can speak!

But, warns Lady Two, he had better not use his tongue for any more lies! Papageno quickly promises never to do so again! He will always remember the lock. In a pleasant trio, the ladies comment:

"If all liars could get a padlock on their mouth... instead of hate, lies, poison—love and friendship would reign!"

Now, at last, comes the magic flute. Lady One gives Tamino the golden flute...a gift from Pamina that will protect him through all dangers. With it he will be able to do anything...make those who are sad, happy...change women-haters into lovers!

Tamino is overjoyed to have such a precious flute. But

Papageno is not too impressed and so "fair ladies I shall take my leave." The Three Ladies have other things in mind. Papageno is to go with the Prince to the castle of Sarastro by order of the Queen!

"No, thank you!"

He has no intention of going along. He's heard from their own lips that Sarastro is "as savage as a tiger!" He would probably roast him for his dinner...or at least throw him to his dogs. Even when they tell him that the Prince would guard him, Papageno says "the devil with the Prince"...his life is too valuable...and, besides, that Prince in the long run would probably take off like a bird. But the ladies pay no attention. Instead, they give him a gift of some toy bells. Well, this perks him up. Chiming bells! Will he be able to play them? Of course! "Silver bells...magic flute...will surely protect you...!"

And so the ladies bid farewell. But Tamino has one more question: how is he going to find Sarastro? In high, almost squeaky voices, the ladies explain that three "young, fair, handsome and wise" boys will go with them and be their guides! They must follow them and do everything that they say. That's it. All call their good-byes...Tamino and Papageno are off on their journey as the scene ends.

In the next scene, we see a rich room in Sarastro's palace. In walks the evil Moor, Monostatos (Mone-oh-STAH-tohs), with Pamina being dragged in by slaves. She is desperate. The Moor announces that her life is ended! The girl is not afraid for herself...she thinks only of her dear mother who will die of grief. Monostatos orders her to be chained. But Pamina would die rather than be Monostatos' prisoner..."a barbarian (high note) who will never let her go!" She faints and falls on a couch. The Moor tells the others to leave him alone with her.

Onto this scene pops Papageno! He wonders where he is. He looks around. Then he hears voices. Why not see what's going on? He goes inside. In a spritely way, he comments about this beautiful young girl...who looks as pale as chalk! Suddenly,

Papageno and Monostatos discover each other! They're both scared out of their wits. Each one thinks the other is certainly the "devil"! With frightened cries, Monostatos runs away. Papageno gets control of himself.

"Am I not foolish to allow myself to become frightened? There are black birds in the world...why not black men? Ah, there...there is Pamina! You, daughter of the Queen of the Night..."

"Who are you?" wonders the girl.

Why, he's been sent by the "Star-bright Queen." Pamina is overjoyed. She thinks that she has heard of Papageno, but has never met him. He gets down to business. He explains that after many years of catching birds for the palace, he's suddenly faced with someone who calls himself a Prince. In short, her mother was so attracted to this Prince that she showed him "your picture"...and ordered him to come to her rescue. He decided to do so as fast as he fell in love with her.

"He loves me? Then why is he taking so long?"

"The Prince sent me ahead to announce his coming."

"You are in great danger! If Sarastro finds you here..."

Papageno comically finishes by saying that he wouldn't have to worry about getting home again! No, he doesn't have a wife waiting for him. He doesn't even have a sweetheart...let alone a wife! He feels like tearing off all his feathers when he thinks that Papageno doesn't yet have a Papagena!

In a steady, measured beat, they sing a short duet. "For someone who wants love...," sings Pamina, "will have a gentle heart." They will both be happy in love, living for love alone. Love takes away all pain. There is nothing finer than to be man and wife... "man and wife, and wife and man...(flowery) a state that is divine!" And after repeating this noble thought, they both go out.

The next scene is brought in with a soft introduction. In a grove, toward the back, are three temples...the Temple of

Wisdom, the Temple of Reason and the Temple of Nature. Soon we meet the Three Boys as they lead Tamino into view.

Here is the path he must take. He must be manly to be victorious. He must be strong, patient and silent!

"Fair children...tell me...will I be able to save Pamina?"

Sweetly they sing that they can't tell him that secret. All they can advise is that he must be manly to be victorious! And with that they leave.

Tamino is again alone. He looks around. He knows that the boys have given him wise ideas that he will take to heart. But he still wonders where he is. What will become of him? Is this the home of the gods? He can see from the temples that Wisdom, Work and Art are the rule. He is going to go through the gate without fear...for his mission is noble...and pure! (His voice is as high as the thought.)

"Tremble...cowardly demons! To save Pamina is my duty!"

So he boldly steps up to the door on the right...but has hardly reached it when a voice inside warns him to stay back. (We hear light violins, then the bass strings.) All right, then he'll try his luck with the door on the left. Stay back, again! So he goes to the middle one and raps on the door. Out comes an important-looking figure known as the "Speaker."

"What do you want, bold stranger? What are you looking for in this sanctuary?"

"The place of Love and Virtue."

Well, this sounds pretty good to the Speaker...but he doesn't think that love and virtue will be Tamino's guide, because he's fired up with death and revenge. That may be, but his vengeance is against the evil demon! Well, he won't find him here.

But Tamino pushes on. Isn't this the place where Sarastro rules? Yes. In the Temple of Wisdom? Yes. In that case, the whole thing is all (high, long note) a two-faced lie! Tamino will go back...never again to see the temples!

The Speaker starts to understand that this young man has received a twisted story. He hates Sarastro because he was told by an unhappy woman that Sarastro is a monster, a tyrant! Oh, so he has been fooled by a woman's story—if only Sarastro would explain away the whole thing. It's certainly plain to Tamino—that the robber tore Pamina from her mother's arms!

That's true. Well, then, has she already been sacrificed? Where is she? But the Speaker's tongue is tied; he is forbidden to say more.

Tamino wonders when he will really know the truth. His voice is doubtful. Solemnly, in a nice melody, the Speaker explains that only when Tamino comes in friendship will the full story be known. In a sweet tune, Tamino, now alone, asks "eternal night...when will my eyes see the light!" Then, deep inside, a chorus is heard: "Soon, soon, young man—or never!" Tamino is now upset. In a loud, impatient voice, he demands to know if his loved one is still alive. The mysterious, heavenly voices answer... "Pamina still lives!"

Tamino is overjoyed. He takes out his magic flute to play a pretty song to the gods...that comes from his heart. He begins to play and at once, all kinds of animals appear to listen! As soon as he stops, they run away. In a flowery way, he sings of how powerful his magic flute must be...that even wild animals come to listen! But his mind is still on his love.

"Only Pamina is not touched...Pamina! Listen, listen to me! No use! Where? Where will I find you?"

But all he hears is Papageno's piping. He sings out in a full, hopeful voice. Maybe he has seen Pamina! Maybe she's coming here with him! Maybe the music will lead him to them! And off he goes.

The scene switches to Pamina and Papageno. She tries to call out to her Tamino, but Papageno wants her to be quiet; his pipes will do the trick. He plays on them...and from off-stage we hear

Tamino's answering tune. In a sweeping melody, the girl and the bird-man sing of their joy. Tamino has heard them! What luck that they have been found! "Come quickly! Come quickly!"

But their luck has run out! In comes the leering Moor with his slaves. He makes fun of her..."come quickly, come quickly!" He gloats that he has caught her; he orders the slaves to bring the iron chains to bind her. Both Pamina and Papageno mournfully note that "it's all over!"

But Papageno isn't through yet. He thinks of the magic bells.

"Ring...ring...pretty bells...sing in their ears..." They work! In an instant Monostatos and his slaves are dancing and singing.

"Those bells so wonderful, Those bells so beautiful! La ra, la ra, la ra... I have never heard the like before!"

Merrily dancing and singing, the Moor and his men "larala" away! This gives the girl and her friend (and Mozart) another chance to moralize. They sing that if all brave men could find such bells...there would be no more trouble, and all would live in harmony. Without such caring, there cannot be happiness on earth!

When they end, a horn fanfare sounds. Voices call, "Long live Sarastro!" Papageno wants to know what this all means; he is quivering and quaking. Pamina cries that this is the end of them; Sarastro is about to arrive. In a frightened tone, Papageno wishes that he were a little mouse so that he could hide, or a small snail so that he could creep into his shell. "My child, what do we say now?" She will tell the truth even though it may be bad for them.

After another fanfare, in comes Sarastro and his following. The chorus sings their welcome...they are his...and long may he wisely rule! He is their High Priest. Pamina falls to her knees. She confesses that she was wrong in trying to escape. But it was because the evil Moor wanted to love her that she was forced to flee.

With great majesty, Sarastro tells her to rise. Even before

he asked her, he knew the secret in her heart. She is deeply in love and, although he will not tell her whom to love, he still will not set her free. His voice is deep. Pamina tries to explain that she is only following her mother's wishes. Sarastro interrupts—her mother is in his power! And that she, Pamina, would be made very unhappy if he allowed her to fall into her mother's hands. Pamina starts to protest that her mother's name sounds sweet to her. She is...

"...a proud woman," says Sarastro.

A *man* must be the one who claims Pamina's heart!

Before anything else is said, Monostatos ushers in Tamino! The two lovers are stunned. They can't believe that they are together—perhaps it's a dream! His arms yearn to hold her. Her arms yearn to hold him. They go to each other...they embrace..."even though it may be the end for them!"

Very dramatically, Monostatos tries to take advantage of this scene. He thinks they have some nerve to act that way...he wants them apart—they go too far! Then he tries to put all the blame for the "stealing" of Pamina on Papageno. To a light violin accompaniment, he goes on to say that it was "this rare bird's trick...to try to steal Pamina!" But he, Monostatos, wasn't fooled...his watchfulness...

"must be rewarded," ends Sarastro.

Then Sarastro calls out that this honorable man should receive (not what Monostatos expects)..."seventy-seven lashes!"

"Ah, Lord, I don't deserve this!"

"Don't thank me," says Sarastro, sarcastically, "it is just my duty!"

Then he orders that the two strangers be led to the Temple of Trials...and that their heads be covered, for first they must be purified. His deep voice ends.

Now follows a quick, rousing chorus, glorious voices...and trumpets...as the act comes to a close.

"When virtue and justice...are everywhere... Then earth will be like heaven...And mortals will be like gods!"

ACT II

To soft, solemn music...and the sound of smooth woodwinds and flutes, the scene opens. There is a forest of palm trees. Sarastro and his priests enter in procession. He stops. Then he announces that today is one of the most important ever. Tamino, son of a king, is to take away his veil and look upon the true light. He is to be watched over and offered the hand of friendship. The First Priest then asks if Tamino is virtuous. Yes. Can he stay silent? Yes. Is he good-hearted? Yes. Three fanfare chords are played.

So...if he is all these things, then he will be given "the gentle maid," Pamina. This is the reason that she was taken from her mother...a woman who thinks too much of herself...who tries to fool her people by trickery and superstition...and who wants to destroy their temple. That will not be! Tamino himself will help them.

The First Priest asks if the great Sarastro believes that Tamino can really pass the tests that he'll have to take...after all, he is a Prince. But Sarastro has no fear about that..."he is more than a Prince, he is a *man*!" So Tamino and Papageno are shown into the courtyard of the temple; Sarastro orders the Speaker to make divine power known to the two young people. Then in a slow, majestic aria, he sings to the Egyptian gods.

"O, Isis and Osiris grant these two the power of your wisdom! You who guide the wanderer's steps give them patience and strength in this hour of danger."

His voice is deep; the chorus repeats this wish. Sarastro asks the gods to reward Tamino and Papageno for their efforts...but if they should fail, then the gods are asked to take them to their resting place. With the chorus adding their voices to the same wish, the scene ends.

It is now night. Papageno and Tamino are led into the temple courtyard by The Three Priests who then leave. It's pitch black. Tamino is the first to speak.

"What a terrible night! Papageno, are you still there?"

"I sure am!"

"Where do you think we are?"

Well, if it wasn't so dark he could tell him, but...(thunder!)

"Hey!" cries Papageno at the noise.

"What's the matter?"

"I don't feel so good!"

"I think you're afraid."

"I'm not afraid...I just have chills up and down my spine."

With another clap of thunder, Papageno is really "cold." Suddenly, priests come in carrying torches.

"Hey there, strangers...what brings you here within our walls?"

"Friendship and love," answers Tamino, nobly.

Yes, Tamino is ready to fight for these ideals even if his life is in danger. After promising that he will take on everything that comes along, the Priest offers him his hand. The Second Priest turns to Papageno. Will he also fight for the sake of Wisdom? Papageno doesn't really want any part of this. He's not a fighting man...and he doesn't actually *need* to be wise. He's just a simple fellow who is happy to have a place to sleep, eat and drink—if he could only catch himself a pretty little wife one of these days...

"You'll never get that unless you take our tests," warns the Second Priest.

"What are they?" asks Papageno, carefully.

"To obey all our orders...and not to fear death itself."

That's it; Papageno decides he'll stay unmarried! But what

if Sarastro could get him a young girl that's just like him in looks and dress? He begins to weaken.

"Like me?" he repeats wistfully. "Is she young?"

"Young and beautiful!"

"And her name?..."

"Papagena!"

This completely startles Papageno. He can't believe his ears.

"Pa...?"

"Papagena," repeats the Priest.

Well, this is something else! He would like to see her—"only because I'm curious..." The Priest agrees. But Papageno is still not sure. What does he have to do, die first? In that case, he'll still stay single! No...he can see her, but he has to have enough willpower not to talk to her. Oh, sure. And so the deal is sealed. Tamino will be able to see Pamina as well...but he, too, must not speak to her. That's part of the trial. Then before the Priests leave, they sing a lively tune warning them that women can be tricky. They had better be careful or their only reward will be death and despair.

When the Priests leave so do the torches, so Tamino and Papageno are once again in total darkness! Papageno can't see a thing..."even with the eyes open!" So Tamino advises him to have patience for it must be the will of the gods. Before Papageno can answer, the Three Ladies appear! They're shocked!

"What? You're here in this dismal place? Never, never, never...will you leave happy!"

Tamino is doomed to die...and so is Papageno! Well, that's going too far for the bird-man! Tamino warns him to be quiet—to remember his vow! Yes, but they're going to die! Still Tamino orders him to be quiet—to remember his vow! Yes, but they're going to die! Still Tamino orders him to be quiet.

The Three Ladies go on to say that the Queen has secretly entered the temple! Papageno can't resist opening his mouth again. To think that the Queen is right there! And so the action goes: Tamino trying to keep his friend quiet, the Three Ladies trying to turn them against the "bad" Priests, our hero not believing them one bit—even if the Queen *did* say so!

"Why do you speak to us so harshly?" they ask.

Tamino signals them that he will not answer. When they turn to Papageno, he can't resist whispering—but he is again ordered to shut up by the Prince! And when he sadly comments that it's really a disgrace the way he can't hold his tongue, Tamino agrees with him.

By now the Three Ladies have about given up. If they won't talk, what's the use? All agree that it takes a strong man who thinks but does not speak. Right then a priest's voice is heard complaining that the "sacred soil has been spoiled"...and that these women should be sent to the devil! That's no sooner said than all three disappear! With a cry, Papageno falls to the ground.

When the Priests appear, they praise Tamino for being strong and manly. But he has a lot more to go through. "So come!"

"Stand up, Papageno," commands the Second Priest.

"I have fainted," calls Papageno.

"Get up! Be a man!"

"If the gods have promised me a Papagena...why do I have to go through all this to get her?"

The Priest ignores that and just tells them to come and follow him!

The setting now changes to a garden where we see Pamina asleep. A ray of moonlight lights her beautiful face. Monostatos is in love with her. He starts toward her as he sings a quick melody. We hear the violins and flutes.

"Everyone feels the joy of love...caressing...holding... loving and kissing...And I have to give up love... Just because a black is ugly, is no heart to be given to me? Am I not of flesh and blood? To live forever without a woman... is truly to be in hell!"

Monostatos goes on to express his love for Pamina. He can't resist the desire to hold her and kiss her. Silently and slowly he starts to go to the sleeping girl. But when her mother, the Queen, suddenly appears, Pamina wakes. The Moor is surprised to hear the girl call the Queen of the Night, "mother"! The Queen, whispering, asks her the whereabouts of the young man she sent to her. When she tells her, the Queen declares that he is doomed! She gives Pamina a shining knife—she is to kill Sarastro! The girl is shocked!

"A vengeful hell beats in my heart," sings the Queen. "Death and despair swirl around me! If you don't kill Sarastro...you are no longer my daughter!"

Her voice, in beautiful *coloratura*, repeats her threat. Then, without words, her voice becomes flowery, colorful. Then she continues. She will renounce her...she will forever be cut off from her...if Sarastro does not die at Pamina's hand!

"Hear me!" she cries, her voice rising. "Gods of revenge...hear a mother's vow!"

She disappears.

Now Monostatos sees his chance. Pamina, to herself, admits that she can't do as her mother wants. What should she do? Monostatos asks her to trust him, as he takes the knife from her.

There is only one way that she can save herself and her mother. How's that? By loving him!

"Now, maiden...yes or no!"

"No!" answers Pamina firmly.

Monostatos is about to strike when in comes Sarastro and holds his arm! The Moor tries to make excuses, but Sarastro simply says that he knows all about it and orders him to go. Monostatos runs off.

Pamina turns to Sarastro to beg him not to punish her mother. Sarastro calms her down. He will show her how he will be avenged.

"In these holy halls," he sings, "vengeance is unknown... when a man is fallen, love shows him what to do."

Then he repeats three times—in a very deep voice—that by the hand of friendship...a man is led—happily—into a better land. Inside the holy walls, where all love each other...there is no room for vengeance...all enemies are forgiven. He ends by saying again and again that whoever is not joyful in learning this lesson...doesn't deserve to be a man. The scene ends.

The next scene is in a large hall. Tamino and Papageno are brought in by two priests. They're still on trial and are told that they must remember one thing, silence. Then they are left alone. After a moment, Papageno can't keep his mouth closed.

"Tamino!"

"Sh-h-h-h!"

"What a life," complains the bird-man, "if I were back in my straw hut, or in the forest, I would at least hear the birds sing!"

"Sh-h-h-h!"

But he can't keep quiet. Can't he even talk to himself? And why can't they speak to each other? Again Tamino tells him to be quiet. So Papageno starts to sing!

He stops just long enough to complain that they don't even give them a drop of water, let alone anything else. As if by magic, an ugly old woman comes in with a large goblet of water!

"Hey, old lady! Is that for me?"

"Yes, my angel!"

"Water," cries Papageno as he gulps it down.

"For sure, my angel," squeaks the old woman.

So Papageno asks her to sit with him—the time is dragging

anyway.

"How old are you?"

"Eighteen years and two minutes!" replies the crone.

Well, he thinks this is a fine joke! He keeps up the fun.

"Do you have a sweetheart?"

"For sure!"

"Is he as young as you are?"

"Not exactly...he's ten years older."

Ten years older? That must make him a fine lover, thinks Papageno. Then he asks her his name.

"Papageno!" comes the answer.

This is too much. Papageno laughs out loud. And where is this "Papageno?" Why right here sitting next to her..."my angel!" He can't believe what she's telling him, and in a fit he tosses the water at her. He demands to know her name! She is just about to tell him when she quickly shuffles off. He doesn't know *what* to make of all this, so he firmly decides that he's not going to say another word!

In come The Three Boys! One has the magic flute, another the bells. Miraculously, a table full of goodies appears! They sing in high, sweet voices.

"Welcome once again...to Sarastro's kingdom! He returns to you the flute and the bells which he had taken."

They invite them to eat and drink...and before they leave, they promise that should they meet for the third time...they will be happily rewarded for showing such courage. To the sound of comic violins...and with a last word of "courage" to Tamino...while they again tell Papageno to be still...they leave.

"Tamino, aren't we going to eat?"

For a reply he gets a tune on the flute. So, let him play his flute, thinks Papageno...I'll be quiet by filling my mouth with good things to eat!

"Ah—what heavenly wine!"

The flute stops. There is Pamina! Joyfully she runs to her love. She heard his flute and came running to its sound. But she notices that Tamino is sad. Hasn't he anything to say to his Pamina? He signals that she should leave. (Remember, he's been sworn to silence.) Pamina doesn't understand. Doesn't he love her anymore? She turns to Papageno. Maybe *he* can explain. But he's got so much food in his mouth that all he can say is, "Hm, hm, hm!"

Sadly, Pamina believes that he, too, will not speak to her. Her dear Tamino...and he wants nothing to do with her. This is worse than death! Slowly, mournfully, to a measured accompaniment, she sings.

"Ah, I feel it...all is now gone...the joys of love are lost!"

Her voice is soft; it flies from note to note in lovely *fioritura*.

"Never again will her heart feel hours of ecstasy!" Her tears are flowing for him alone. If he does not answer her call of love...there will only be left...

"...the peace (high, long note) of death!"

Pamina leaves sorrowfully.

The next scene takes place inside a closed temple room. Sarastro and his priests sing a full-voiced chorus to Isis and Osiris. Darkest night has given way to the rays of the sun! Soon a noble youth shall know a new life and become part of them. Then, in a chanting way they end up by noting that his "spirit is strong, his heart is pure...soon he will be worthy..." Here, Tamino is led in by a priest.

Sarastro compliments him on his actions so far, but he still has two more tests to pass. Sarastro calls for Pamina. He takes her hand. Pamina is confused and wants only Tamino. He is waiting for her, only to give her a last good-bye! They meet but cannot come together. Pamina wonders if they will ever see each other again. She's told that they will...and in happiness. The gods will protect Tamino.

Pamina thinks that if he loved her as much as she loves him he wouldn't be so calm about leaving her. Sarastro assures her that he will be forever faithful; Tamino repeats what Sarastro has just said. Now the time to part has arrived. And with the two lovers calling their farewells...while being assured that they will soon meet again in happiness...the lovers depart.

What's this? Papageno is now alone. He calls after the Prince. Is he going to be left by himself? He wishes he knew where he was! When he gets to the door through which Tamino left, a voice commands him to back away. He tries the door where he had come in. "Stay back!" Now he can't go forward or backward. He starts to cry. In comes a priest.

> "Man! You deserve to wander forever in the darkest bowels of the earth..."

But the merciful gods have taken away his punishment...although he will never know the joys of being one of the chosen. That's all right with Papageno—there'll be a lot more just like him. To him a nice glass of wine would be just as heavenly! A large glass magically appears!

> "Hurray! Here it is!"

> "Don't you want anything else in the world?" asks the Priest.

Papageno does have a strange feeling in his heart. He thought he wanted something—but he can't remember what it was! Merry bells introduce Papageno's song.

> "A young maiden or a little wife...that's what Papageno wishes. Oh, a soft dove would be happiness for me! Then more delicious would be food and drink... Then I'd be as good as a Prince, Be able to live much wiser, And feel like I was in paradise!"

To the happy sound of bells he goes on. All he wants is a young maiden or a little wife, and if he doesn't have one for his own...he'll just die of sadness. He continues with his bouncy song, repeating his wishes for "a little wife." And if he doesn't get one, he'll be destroyed! But if he gets just one maiden's kiss...he'll be born again! The full orchestra ends his wistful song.

In pops the old lady dancing around with her walking stick.

"I'm here already, my angel!"

"Did you have pity on me?"

Papageno thinks that's very nice of her. The old woman then explains that if he promises to be forever faithful to her, he will see how tenderly his little wife will love him.

"Not so fast, dear angel! This kind of thing needs a lot of thought."

But the old lady warns him not to be too long. He had better give her his hand or he'll be in prison forever! Prison? Yes...he'll be living without a sweetheart, and never see the world again. That sounds pretty bad. He figures that he'd rather have this old dame than nothing at all. So he agrees—she has his word that he will always be faithful. Then, to himself, he murmurs, "as long as he doesn't find anyone better looking."

"Do you promise?"

"I promise!"

At that word the old lady suddenly turns into a young girl dressed exactly like him! Papageno is astounded! He can hardly talk. There she is!

"Pa-Pa Papagena!"

He's just about to grab her when a priest comes in and tells him to back away! Oh, yeah? Before he draws back, may the earth swallow him up! No sooner said than done! Papageno sinks out of sight! His last words are "Oh, ye gods!" as the drums rolls.

The scene changes to a garden. There are The Three Boys. They tell us that soon the sun will shine as morning arrives. Suspicions will disappear and man will be wise. They ask that sweet contentment join with them...enter once more the hearts of men...then will the earth be a heavenly place...and mortals be the same as gods.

Boy One sees Pamina. She is desperate. She is out of her mind. She suffers from a love that is not returned. Here she comes! The boys decide to stay out of sight and watch what she is going to do.

Pamina appears with a dagger in her hand! Is this to be her bridegroom? This is the way her grief will be ended! The boys are startled to hear her words. The poor girl is close to going insane! They realize that she doesn't know what she is doing. They call to her. But she is too far gone. She wants to die because the man she still loves has left her in sorrow. She points to the knife. It was given to her by her mother!

"God will punish her if she commits suicide," warn the boys.

She would rather die from the knife than from the pangs of love. She thinks of her mother. It is because of her that she is suffering...her mother's curse follows her still. She is about to kill herself when the boys stop her. If she goes through with this, it will kill the man she loves...for he loves no one but her!

"What? He returns my love?...Yet he turned away from me...why wouldn't he speak to me?"

Well, all three boys explain faster and faster...they can't give away that secret...but they can show her where he is. She'll be surprised to find that his heart belongs to her...for her he's not afraid to die. Then they all sing that two hearts aflame with love no human power can part...for they are protected by the gods!

The next scene is introduced by full chords, then violins and bass strings with a regular rhythm. There are two giant mountains...one with a flowing waterfall, the other spewing out flames. We see Tamino with two men in black armor. The Armored Men declare that he who goes along this way, a path full of dangers, must pass fire, water, air and earth. When he has overcome the fear of death, then he will have risen from earth and be as if in heaven. He will see the light and be blessed with the mysteries of Isis. Heroically, Tamino cries that he does not fear death. He is ready for the trials.

Then he hears Pamina's voice from inside.

"Tamino, stop! I must see you!"

"What's that I hear? Pamina's voice?"

"Yes, yes, that is Pamina's voice," sing the Armored Men.

With all voices blending, Tamino rejoices at the thought that Pamina may join him...no fate can separate them—even if they are doomed to die!

"Am I allowed to speak to her?"

When the men agree, Tamino's voice rises in joy at the thought that they will see each other again. Together they would enter the temple, hand in hand—and she would neither fear night nor death...she would be worthy of being blessed. The violins introduce Pamina as she comes in led by the Second Priest. The two lovers are ecstatic! They will be together whatever the test—*there* are the gates of terror! She will always be at his side...and love will be her guide.

"You will play on your magic flute," she sings—her voice happily hitting a high note.

It will protect them on their way; a flute carved by her father from the heart of a thousand-year-old oak, in a magic moment...through lightning, thunder, storm and tempest!

"Come now and play the flute so it will cheer us along the horrible road."

And so Pamina and Tamino happily sing that music will guard them as they go through the "shadow of death." The Armored Men sing along with them. A graceful flute melody introduces a light duet. Both lovers dream of how they are saved from both fire and water by the wondrous flute. We hear it as both are happy that the gods, Isis herself, give them blessings. Horns and a triumphal full orchestra join a chorus of priests who sing from within that the "noble pair" have passed the tests and they are to be given the rites of Isis!

"Come, enter the temple!"

On this stirring note we leave this scene and find ourselves alone with Papageno. He is playing on his pipes. He feels as low as anybody can. He is crying for his Papagena! His little wife, his dove, his sweetheart has left him—all because he spoke to her. Between the delicious wine he drank and his love for his little woman, his heart is all on fire.

"Papagena, my heart's little woman! Papagena, my dear little dove! It's no use, she is lost to me!"

So he decides that the only way out of his misery is to hang himself! He's going to hang from "this tree."

"Good night...cruel world! You have treated me badly...and since you have not given me a beautiful child...all is over, I will die...lovely young girl, think of me!"

But he isn't really too keen on all this. Won't someone try to stop him? Won't anybody say "yes" or "no"? Not a word. All right then, up he'll go! He'll put an end to his life! No, he'll wait awhile—but only until he counts "one, two, three." He blows on his pipes again. This is a tough decision to make. But he starts in. "One!" Then slowly. "Two!" Even slower (hoping that someone, somewhere will stop him). "Th-r-e-e!" Nothing. O.K. then, that's it! There's nothing to hold him back! "Good night, cruel world," he says, sadly...as he begins to put the rope around his neck.

"Stop it, O Papageno, and be smart; you only have one life to live—and that should be enough."

There are The Three Boys—just in time! Papageno couldn't be happier. They're right, he thinks, but if they felt as he did, they would also go after girls. They pay no attention to that. They just tell him to play on his magic bells and they will bring back his little woman! Dumbbell! He forgot all about them!

And so to the cheerful sound of the magic bells, Papageno calls on them to bring back his loved one!

"Now, Papageno, look around!" cry The Three Boys.

And there she is! Papageno is stunned out of his mind. Papagena is filled with wonder.

"Pa-Pa-Pa-Pa-Pa-Pa- Papagena!" he stutters.

"Pa-Pa-Pa-Pa-Pa-Pa- Papageno!" she stutters.

"Are you really mine?"

"I am really yours!"

Oh, how happy they will be! And if the gods don't forget them, and let them have some loving children, then they will love their little children!

"First a little Papageno!"

"Then a little Papagena!"

They'll be full of happiness with many Papagenos and Papagenas. On that happy thought they end, along with the full orchestra. . .and they quickly leave.

Once again we see the underground vault. Sneaking around to creepy music is the evil Monostatos and the evil Queen with her Ladies. The Moor warns them to be still, still, still. Soon they will be in the temple. Will the Queen keep her promise to give him her daughter as his wife? She will. Good. They must be quiet! He hears a terrible sound—like thundering and a waterfall. The women hear it too. Monostatos explains that the others are now in the Temple Hall. That is where they'll attack them and get their revenge by ridding the earth of "those pious ones," with fire and the mighty sword. They will all disappear into eternal night! The voices and orchestra are strong. There is thunder and lightning.

Suddenly, the whole scene is flooded with blazing light! Sarastro is there in all his glory! Tamino and his beloved are dressed in priestly gowns; on each side are the Egyptian Priests. The Three Boys are holding bouquets of flowers. It is the Temple of the Sun! Chords ring out.

"The rays of the sun drive away the night...and destroy the power of the evil ones!" declares Sarastro in his deep voice.

He is very majestic. The chorus of priests sing to the sound of lively violins. They hail the new members of the holy order. Night has been conquered. Thanks to Isis and Osiris! Might is victorious...and crowns beauty and wisdom forever! The last words are sung with heavenly voices...then join the music's powerful ending...as the beautiful, colorful scene comes to a dramatic close.

THE CURTAIN FALLS

As we have said, Mozart was a Mason. But he was a devout Roman Catholic as well. In both cases, good must triumph over evil. And so it does, in this, his last opera. Although the plot has been called an odd mixture of old-fashioned German comedy and high-sounding moral ideas, it all comes together through the genius of his splendid music. This is truly one opera that has to be heard to be fully appreciated.

Why the Egyptian setting? One reason is that people in those days were interested in the mystery of that part of the world. It also gave Mozart—through Sarastro—a good way to talk about his love of the goodness of man. (The Temple of Isis is probably Freemasonry itself.) Tamino, too, was Mozart—always looking to better himself...to follow "the path of virtue." On the other side was Papageno. That's Mozart's light-hearted Austrian side—the weaker part of his character that always longed for a proper wife.

Mozart never did get that. He married Constanze Weber, although he first was in love with her sister, Aloysia. She forgave him for his flirtations with others; she helped him with his career;

she spent a lot of his money. He loved her in his way and went crazy when he had to be away from her. One of the things for which Constanze will always be remembered is that she saved most of her husband's works by selling them to Andre, a publishing house in Frankfurt. She also supplied her second husband, George Nikolaus von Nissen, with facts about Mozart so that he could write the first story of his life.

As with Wagner in his *Tristan*, Mozart thought of death as his "true best friend." But he wasn't too thrilled by something that happened in Vienna before his *Magic Flute* was finished. One day a stranger, dressed all in gray, knocked on his door and handed him an order to write a *Requiem Mass*—a Mass for the dead! Then he disappeared without a word. Mozart was sure that he had been approached by Death itself. He knew he was deathly ill. As he worked he was convinced that he was writing *his own Requiem!* Meanwhile, he began to think that he was being poisoned. His health, never any good, really began to go down hill. But the Mass had to be finished first! Weak and sick, he tried to end it before he died. He couldn't. (While in bed he would look at his watch and tell those with him just what part of *The Magic Flute* was being done at that moment.) But then on December 5, 1791, at the young age of thirty-five—about two months after his finest opera had opened—Mozart died of typhoid fever. From Mozart's last notes, a pupil named Sussmeyer completed what the great composer had in mind. And the mysterious one? An employee from the Count von Walsegg who wanted to say that he wrote the Requiem! That's why he told his servant to keep everything secret.

And so, on a cold, rainy morning, the man whom Wagner himself called "music's genius of light and love" was taken to St. Mark's churchyard to be buried in a pauper's grave. No one was there, not even his wife. Much later she went to put a cross on his grave, but couldn't find it; to this day it is unknown.

But the boy baptized Johannes Chrysostomus Wolfgangus Theophilus Mozart lives on. (Theophilus became the German

Gottlieb and then the Latin Amadeus; his signature was always Wolfgang Amade Mozart.)

The Magic Flute was first heard in America, in English, at the Park Theatre in New York, April 17, 1833. It wasn't until November 10, 1862, that it was performed uncut and in the original language at the German Opera House, also in New York City. The Metropolitan did it finally (in Italian) on March 30, 1900, and starred the great Marcella Sembrich, Emma Eames, Dippel and Plancon.

There will always be wonder when we think of Mozart. Just as recently as 1982, another symphony was discovered in Odense, Denmark! It is a three part, ten instrument work that he wrote when he was only nine years old!—another amazing piece to be added to the more than 40 symphonies and at least 626 works written in his too short lifetime.

But we must be on our way. Leaving ancient Egypt, where our comic love-birds Papageno and his Papagena and Tamino with Pamina will live happily ever after, we fly in a fairy tale way— like Peter Pan—to a deep forest in ancient Germany. Just as Mozart had used folk-music and characters in his *Flute*, another composer by the unlikely name of Engelbert Humperdinck reached out to authentic German folklore to create the wonderland opera, *Hansel and Gretel*.

And since we began this storybook with an opera—*Die Fledermaus*—that is traditionally played on New Year's Eve, why not close, for now, with one that is traditionally performed all over the world at Christmastime!

> *It might be nice to talk a little about Christmas and how so many of the things that are done today at that jolly time of the year came from Germany; for instance, the gingerbread house that we will "see" when we get into the story of the two children. The decorations of evergreens and the log on the fire came from the German pagans long ago. Although it was St. Boniface who is supposed to have put up*

the first tree, it was the German Martin Luther who put on the candles many years later.

Of course, we can't overlook Charles Dickens famous story A Christmas Carol *that showed us the holiday in England. While here in America, the classic poem "Twas The Night Before Christmas" by Clement Moore actually created Santa Claus as we know him today. But we can't forget that the most famous Christmas song of all time is "Silent Night, Holy Night," composed for the little church of Oberndorf, Germany, sung for the first time on Christmas Day in 1818.*

In Germany there had always been tales about heroes and dragons and dwarfs and many characters that became part of their folk history. One day Jacob and Wilhelm Grimm decided to gather as many of these ancient stories as they could, and they published them as *Grimm's Fairy Tales*. One of them was the adventures of Hansel and Gretel.

For years the opera stage—especially in Germany—was "owned" by Richard Wagner. His kind of heavy music and drama was the chief entertainment in his native land as well as in other opera houses. When he died, there did not seem to be anything or anybody to take his place. However, Humperdinck had come along (they met in Naples in March of 1880) and had actually been asked by Wagner to help him put on his great opera *Parsifal*. . . which the young twenty-five year old composer was very happy to do. He worked with Wagner for several years; he was teacher to his son Siegfried; and when the famous composer left an opening in the world of opera, Humperdinck was there to fill the gap. Naturally, he could never completely fill those big shoes, but by this time the German people had had about enough of deep, dark works so that when *Hansel and Gretel* opened in the Weimer Court Theatre on the evening of December 23, 1893, it was welcomed like a ray of sunshine and became *the* Christmas opera everywhere.

Again we hear about *Singspiel*. That's the way it all began. Humperdinck's sister, Adelheid Wette (who became the story writer of the opera), had asked him to compose some songs for a little children's play. It started as a *Song-Spoken* work that grew and grew until it became the full opera we know today.

Although Humperdinck's music was influenced by Wagner, he didn't imitate him. Instead, he wrote music that was original and that bridged the time between Wagner and his true successor, Richard Strauss. And we are charmed. . .as much as the children. . .by the lovely German nursery rhymes that we'll hear. In fact, other children's tunes have become so popular that youngsters sing them today. But there's more. What *Hansel and Gretel* has that's the same as in the "fairy-tale," *The Magic Flute*, is the struggle between good and evil! Just as there was an "evil spirit"—the Queen of the Night—*we* have a wicked Witch. Just as Tamino and Pamina had to go through tests to come out winners, so do Hansel and Gretel. And just as the lovers are richly rewarded in the end, so are brother and sister, as we shall soon see.

It is the night before Christmas Eve, the audience has settled in their seats—and coming up to conduct is the already word-famous composer—young, twenty-nine year old, Richard Strauss! The lights dim; the first performance is about to begin.

7

HANSEL und GRETEL

(HAHN-zel oond GREH-tel)

ACT I

The overture opens with quiet, peaceful music that pictures the old forest and the little house. As it continues it swells from time to time; then horns that play a few notes of what is known as the "Children's Prayer," disappear then come back. We hear the *celeste*. . .then a lively tune that sounds like a folk-dance. Violins become louder and louder, cymbals clash; the happy theme is repeated—then peace returns, horns sound. . .leading to a long, soft close.

The room of the cottage is open to us so we can see Hansel making another broom; his father, the broom maker, is off trying to sell some of them. Gretel is near the fireplace knitting a stocking. There is a cheerful introduction, and then Gretel sings a light, happy song.

> "Susie, dearest Susie what's rustling in the straw? The geese are running barefoot, and have no shoes..."

She goes on to explain that the shoe-maker has leather but not the upper part, so that's why the poor geese don't have any...

Hansel interrupts.

> "Even so! They'll have to go barefoot!"

> "...shoes!" ends up Gretel.

Hansel (sung by a girl; *mezzo-soprano*) continues the same tune saying that they're in trouble. Who'll give them some money for sugar and bread? If he sells his bed and uses straw instead...he won't be stuck by any feather, or bitten by any...

Before he has a chance to finish, Gretel interrupts complaining of "biting hunger." Hansel agrees. He wishes that their mother would come home. They have had nothing to eat but stale bread. Gretel, in her *lyric soprano* voice, reminds him (in a sweet melody) that father always says that when things are at their worst, "God...reaches out his hand!"

That's nice to hear, thinks Hansel, but it doesn't help his hunger. Then he dreams of how long it's been since they've tasted pancakes and "butter bread." He starts to go on, but Gretel covers his mouth and sings that he should'nt be so down-hearted...he shouldn't grumble so much. Then, picking up a broom, she pretends to sweep the "grumbler" out of the house.

Both join in the tune. Hansel says that he can't stand it anymore...always working, being hungry. While his sister, still sweeping, calls him a complainer...and she'll chase him out of the house, even though her own stomach is rumbling with hunger.

And so they play along...until Hansel, too, agrees to chase

away the "horrible creature" with the sad face.

"All right!" cries Gretel.

"If you don't grumble anymore...I'll tell you a secret," she whispers.

Hansel just loves secrets! Listen and he will be happy. Look at the pot of milk that a neighbor gave them! When Mother comes home, she will make them rice pudding!

Well, that's all he has to hear. He looks at the wonderful pot with its creamy goodness...and sticks his finger in it for a taste! Gretel is shocked. He should be ashamed of himself. He'd better take his finger out and get back to work. She keeps on scolding him. If things aren't "right" by the time Mother comes home, things will go bad for the lazy ones.

"Work?" sings Hansel. "That's not what I like to do...let's dance and play instead!"

"Dancing? Dancing?" sings Gretel in a high voice. "I would love that too!"

So she suggests that they dance to the happy dancing song that Grandmother taught them. She begins by clapping her hands. Then to a folk-tune she goes on.

"Little brother, come, dance with me...
first the right foot, then the left...
all around—it isn't hard!"

Hansel tries to follow, but he's not very good. Yet he'd like to learn. Gretel shows him the way; Hansel does the same.

"With the feet, tap, tap, tap...
with the hands, clap, clap, clap...
Once there, once here,
Round about, it isn't hard!"

Gretel is surprised and pleased that Hansel has learned so well. She goes on.

"With your little head, nod, nod, nod...
with your little fingers, tick, tick, tick,

Once there, once here,
Round about, it isn't hard!''

By now they're really getting into the spirit of it all. Gretel shows him how to join arms as they step around. In a duet, which opens with Gretel's lyrical *coloratura*, they sing of how they are not friends of sadness...that they want to be jolly...they love to dance and frolic...and don't like being alone. Happier and happier, they start a ring-around...Hansel claims that Gretel has a hole in her stocking. She sings that he's just teasing her. Anyway, Mother will knit a new one! Faster and faster they whirl about until they both fall down.

Suddenly, there's Mother! Well, what's this? The children don't know what to say. Each one tries to blame the other. But Gertrude will have none of it. How dare they shout and sing, dance and jump—instead of working! Is that the thing to do while their parents work and worry from morning till night?

"Take that!" she cries, as she boxes Hansel's ear.

She looks around to see what they have finished. Hansel didn't complete his brooms, Gretel didn't finish the sock. Angrily, she starts to take a stick to both those "lazybones." But just as she tries, she knocks the crock of milk off the table! It breaks on the floor! What will she ever do for dinner? Hansel can't help snickering.

That's too much for his mother, and she chases him out of the house. Then turning to Gretel, she shoves a basket at her and orders her to go into the woods to pick some strawberries. "Just wait till Father comes home!"

She warns Gretel to bring it back full—or else. Her voice reaches a high note. She tiredly sits on the chair at the table. She despairs about the broken jug and spilled milk. "Blind anger always brings bad luck." If the Lord would only send them some money. There's not a crumb of bread...nothing...and only water to drink. Her story is sad, followed by the low strings. She puts her head down on her arms...and with a last call to the Lord, she falls off to sleep.

Far off we hear a happy voice singing to a slow melody.

"Rallalala, rallalala...Mother, I'm here!
Rallalala, rallalala...bringing happiness and glory!"

Peter's voice is getting closer. He sings about being poor with a hole in his purse...and a bigger one in his stomach. "Hunger is the best cook!" He shows up at the window, then comes in happily delivering a basket. He's feeling no pain—having stopped off at the local bar—-and so he keeps on singing. The rich people can always get food, but the poor have nothing to eat. Lazily he continues his "rallalala," claiming that hunger is the best cook...while *Kümmel* (a liquor) is his favorite drink!

As he puts the basket down, he gives the sleeping woman a kiss. She wants to know who the noise-maker is that woke her up with all the "rallalalas." Peter claims it was the "wild beast" in his stomach...a growly beast such as hunger...that "bites and scratches." His wife comments that it seems that the wild beast is pretty drunk. She pushes him away as, tipsily, he tries to kiss her again. But he has a surprise for her.

"Let's see...what there is to eat...," says he, proudly.

Sadly, Gertrude remarks that the plates are empty and so is the cellar—and they have no money.

"Rallalala, rallalala," sings Peter. "Look, Mother—how do you like all of this?"

From the basket Peter begins to take out one good thing after another! In shocked surprise, Gertrude can't believe her eyes. Butter and bacon, flour and sausages, fourteen eggs—all come out of the basket. But that's not all. Here come the beans, onions—and, hallelujah!—even a quarter of a pound of coffee! Gertrude hits a high note. Peter turns the basket over and out roll some potatoes! Then to the same rollicking melody, they start to sing and dance around the cottage. But Peter can't wait to tell her what happened.

It seems that outside of the forest there are big plans for fairs, weddings and jubilees. So, there's bound to be lots of sweeping, scrubbing and polishing needed. Going from house to house, Peter called out, "Buy brooms! Good sweepers! Fine brushes! Cobweb cleaners!" And that's how he sold everthing at top prices! As the same happy tune that we heard before is playing in the background, Gertrude and Peter begin to drink to their health.

"To the broommakers!"

But then a thought crosses his mind. "Wait a minute—where are the children?" Gertrude wishes that she knew. All she does know is that because of Hansel she broke the jug. Although Peter is angry at hearing this, he still thinks that it was stupid of her to get so angry that the milk was spilled. He asks about the children again. The kettle drums rumble.

"As far as I know, they are at the Ilsenstein!" declares Gertrude.

"At the Ilsenstein? Are you crazy?" Peter cries. "Suppose they're lost in the forest. . .at night, without stars or moonlight!"

"Heavens!"

To mysterious, fearful music Peter asks,

"Don't you know that shudderingly, gloomy place? Don't you realize that the Evil One lives there?"

Gertrude doesn't know what he means—"Evil One"! He's talking about *the gobbling witch*! Gertrude is stunned! The gobbling witch! The bass strings play as Peter picks up a broom. Gertrude wonders what good the broom will do.

To a heavy, somber beat Peter explains that witches *ride* on brooms. An old witch that lives in the woods was given her power from the devil himself! At night (the music gets louder and louder), when no one sees her, she rides out on her witch's hunt. But what does he mean when he calls her the "gobbling witch?"

Well, during the day she lures children to her crispy, crackly, crunchy house for a "witch's feast." With magic cakes she catches the cake-eating children...pushes them into the hot oven, and soon out come brown gingerbread kids!

"And the gingerbread children?" asks Gertrude, shakily.

"They're gobbled up!"

"By the witch?"

"By the witch!"

Gertrude is horrified. She calls to heaven for help. She can't stand it anymore—she must find the children. And with that she runs from the house, with Peter calling and running after her. As the orchestra sounds a chord, the strings play to the end, and the curtain falls.

ACT II

It opens to wild music...forest sounds...kettle drums...violins rise, then things soften; we hear the horns play quietly...violins end sweetly.

It is toward sunset. Gretel is sitting making a crown out of some roses. The mountain, Ilsenstein, looms behind; the children are deep in the thick woods. While Hansel is in the bushes looking for strawberries, Gretel is singing a little song. With a child's *lyric* voice, she sings a slow tune that also has quick short notes. It is a nursery rhyme.

"A little man stands in the woods still and silent;
he wears a purple little coat.
Say, who is this little man who stands in the woods
alone with his little purple coat?"

The little man stands in the woods on one leg...and on his head he has a little black hat. She wonders who he could be? She gets no answer because Hansel breaks in with a big "Hooray!" His basket is full of strawberries; won't his mother be glad!

Gretel, too, is proud of her beautiful circle of flowers and tries to put it on Hansel's head. What? Boys don't wear such things—only girls. He places it on Gretel and tells her that she looks like the Queen of the Woods! This calls for make-believe. Hansel kneels and says she not only should have sceptre and crown...but the basket of strawberries, too. But she's not to eat them!

Just then a cuckoo is heard singing in a tree. The children imitate his call. They know that cuckoos have the bad habit of raiding other birds' nests to rob the eggs. Thinking of that, Gretel pushes a ripe strawberry into Hansel's mouth. He loves it. In fact, they both are getting themselves into deep trouble by eating one after the other as they mimic the cuckoo. Quicker and quicker they go until finally Hansel empties the last few berries into his mouth!

In a frightened voice—with violins to match—Gretel scolds Hansel.

"What have you done, you lummox!"

But he's not going to take the whole blame...after all, she ate quite a few as well. What's she fussing about? But Gretel is worried. She wants to look for more. It's too late—night is beginning to fall, and Hansel knows they wouldn't be able to see even a leaf, let alone strawberries.

"Oh, Hansel, Hansel!" she cries. "What are we to do? How could we have been so stupid?"

They know now that they should not have stayed out so long. We hear the cuckoo again. It has become a frightening sound...along with the rustling of the leaves in the trees! Hansel doesn't help matters very much. We hear the violins sweep along.

"Do you know what the forest is saying?

'Children, children...aren't you afraid?'"

The orchestra sounds gloomy as Hansel realizes that he can't find the way home! His sister begins to panic. He tries to be brave—what a scaredy-cat she is! She feels that something terrible will happen. She sees a "shimmer" over there in the dark. It's just a grove of white birch trees. What about that awful face in the swamp? Just a stump! She sees a light! It's only a firefly. Hansel has tried to calm her down; now he decides to give a loud shout.

"Who's there?" he calls, cupping his hands.

"...There!" comes back the hollow sound.

At the echoes and the sound of the cuckoo, Hansel and Gretel grab each other. They're terrified! Their imaginations run wild. Timidly, Gretel wonders if there is someone there. "There...," comes back the echo...again the cuckoo.

Gretel, holding on to Hansel, is sure that someone is out there. The forest is beginning to look like a ghost as the mist of the night creeps up. The music gets shrill along with Gretel's voice.

"They're coming, the white fog-women.
See how they wave to us and look so threatening.
They're coming, they're coming to catch us!
Father! Mother! Oh, Oh!"

All of a sudden the mood changes. The violins play softly...as a little gray man comes out of the mist. He has a knap-sack on his back. He's pleasant and friendly as he tells them that he's the little Sandman who loves little children. (This part, too, is done by a *soprano* in a gentle, peaceful voice.) From his bag he takes two grains of sand and sprinkles them into their eyes— "sst, sst!" Now they will fall asleep, and the stars will shine and angels on high will bring them sweet dreams.

"So dream, little children, dream...," says the Sandman, as he softly tiptoes away.

Hansel sleepily comments that the "Sandman was here." Gretel suggests that they say their evening prayers. She sounds sleepy, too. They kneel. Together they sing a slow melody...and as they come to a close, their voices become higher before they finally give way to restful sleep.

"Evenings, when I go to sleep,
Fourteen angels come around me:
Two at my head,
Two at my feet,
Two on my right,
Two on my left,
Two to cover me,
Two to wake me,
Two to point the way to Paradise."

And so they drop off clasped in each others arms. Then out of the darkness we see a brilliant light. Miraculously, the mist comes together to make a heavenly stairway. There are the angels! They walk down and put themselves exactly where the children said. The others join hands and dance around them. As the light becomes dazzling, the orchestra becomes stronger, led by high violins... and then the curtain falls.

ACT III

The next morning the children are still asleep. We hear a perky tune... horns, woodwinds, bells and the thin sound of the oboe. There is some dramatic music with full orchestra and soon a harp that introduces the little Dew Man. (This is also sung by a *soprano*.)

He carefully sprinkles a few drops of dew from a flower onto the sleepyheads. At the same time he sings about how he gets up with the sun, and from east to west he knows who is lazy and who is not. He makes the sound of a bell... "ding, dong, ding, dong!" He explains that he comes with the golden sunshine to wake everybody and everything up with "cool dew."

"Get up, sleepyheads, awake...
the bright day is already laughing!"

Once more he bids them to awaken, and then his voice fades as he scurries away.

Gretel is the first one to wake up. She wonders where she is. . .whether she's dreaming or awake. She notices that she's under a fir tree. . .and up in the branches she hears the soft chattering and chirping of birds.

"You dear birds, dear birds, good morning," she cries in a high voice.

Then she turns to Hansel who has decided he wants more sleep. All right, she'll soon wake *him*! She sings right into his ear!

"Tire-lire-li! It's not early anymore!
The lark has sung. . .and has flown away. . .
Tire-lire-li. . ." Her voice is a bright *coloratura*.

Well, this sure awakens him in a hurry. He jumps up and crows like a rooster. Gretel joins in. They're having a merry time. Hansel feels so good; never has he slept so soundly. His sister, too—and she had a wonderful dream! So did Hansel! Gretel hurries on to tell him all about it. . .the angels, the singing, the golden ladder—all of it. Her brother thinks that there must have been at least fourteen angels! And he saw them go—there! As he turns, he sees a marvelous house through the disappearing mist!

Why, it seems to be made of cakes and pastries—and it smells so good! There it is, the Witch's House. So inviting to children. . .with pancakes and tarts. . .sugar windows. . .raisins along the roof—and miracle of miracles—a gingerbread fence! Together they sing a pretty rhyme telling all that they see.

"I wonder what Wood Princess might live there!"

If only the princess would invite them into that lovely little house. They could have cakes and wine. . .and who knows what else. Hansel can't resist. He wants to go inside. But Gretel thinks he's gone out of his mind. After all, who knows who really is in that house? But he can't believe that such a "smiling house". . .a house that the angels must have shown them, could be harmful. It doesn't take Gretel long to agree! So like two little mice, with the right mousy music behind them, they tiptoe to the house and break off a piece of cake. From inside they hear a voice!

"Nibble, nibble, little mouse, who's that nibbling my little house?"

What can that be? Hansel is so startled he drops his cake. Gretel thinks it's the wind. That's fine with him! She picks up the piece and tastes it. Hansel takes a bite too. They love it! To a catchy little tune they sing...

"Hey, hey...Oh delicious cake. I feel as if I were already in heaven!"

They're in ecstasy. Everything is so delicious. Maybe a pastry-maker lives here. What a joke on him! Hansel calls out that he'd better watch out because a little mouse is making a hole in his house. He takes a big chunk out of the wall! Again a voice is heard asking the same question. But the children pay no attention. To them it's the wind..."the heavenly wind!" But their joy is soon to end.

Without the children seeing her, the wicked witch has sneaked out of the house and is about to capture Hansel. When she's close enough, she quickly throws a rope around his neck! Then she laughs her witch's laugh...as Hansel fights to be free. Why, she *likes* the idea that they have come to visit her. She just adores "dear children so round and fat!" She is, "Rosina Daintymouth...innocent as a little child." She loves small children so much—"she could eat them up!"

Hansel doesn't want any part of this ugly old woman. He struggles to get away. But the witch continues to try to lure them into her house. There she will have chocolate, tarts, marzipan, cakes filled with whipped cream, johnnycakes and ladyfingers— *and rice pudding*. It's on the stove. And then there are raisins and figs, almonds and dates...just waiting for them! Her voice is very high.

"I won't go with you, ugly woman!" shouts Hansel.

"You are much too friendly," says Gretel, suspiciously.

Still, the witch keeps on. She wants the little "mice" to come into her house. She tries to drag Hansel inside. She'll be *so* nice to them! Gretel wants to know what she is going to do with Hansel. Well, she'll feed him all kinds of wonderful things...until he's tender and tasty—and then she'll whisper into his ear and a great treat will be his!

Hansel doesn't believe a word. He has already taken off the rope. In a whisper he tells Gretel that they must run away. And that's just what they start to do when the witch waves her magic wand, and they are stopped in their tracks!

"Stop! Hocus pocus!...You move and the river will get you! I put a spell on you with my evil eye!"

Not only that, but the end of her wand starts to shine! This will really help her to put them in her power...they're hypnotized! The voice echoes. She orders Hansel to march into a cage. "Hocus, pocus, bonus locus, malus locus, hocus pocus...," and in he goes. Now she turns to the stiff and staring Gretel. In her gravelly voice, she asks her to "be nice."

Hansel will soon be fat...because she will feed him almonds and raisins. Gretel mustn't leave while she goes into the house to get these goodies. Gretel cries that that witch gives her the shivers!

"Gretel! Psst! Don't talk so loud!" calls Hansel.

Well, he's not as much under a spell as the wicked witch thinks. He instructs Gretel to be smart and watch all that the witch does...and to make believe to do everything that she asks. Here she comes!

The witch is busily taking some almonds and raisins to Hansel. As she goes by she "unstiffens" Gretel with her magic wand. She wants her to quickly go into the house to set the table...so that everything will be ready for her witch's "little mouth." She'd better do a good job of it or she'll lock Gretel up too! She cackles to show that she means it. When she gets to the cage, Hansel pretends to be asleep. She's disgusted.

"That lummox is asleep...how young people can sleep!"

All right, sleep away, "good sheep." She'll take care of "cute, tender and round" Gretel first! The "maid" is just made for her "witch's mouth"! She opens the big oven and takes a sniff. We hear the full orchestra, the kettle drums. She chortles over her plan to have Gretel look inside, and then she'll push her in...and then—"bang"—the door shuts with a "clang"! And in her magic oven, Gretel will turn into fine gingerbread. She's tickled with herself for being so crafty. "He he he!" She's so overjoyed with the thought that she grabs a broom and, to cheery music and the sound of the *celeste* bells, she rides up and all around the house. All the while she sings about "hop, hop, hop" and "clop, clop, clop" on her horsey broom. Her nonsense song tells how she rides all night and down through the chimney...and finally ends her flying in the morning. "Prr! Broomstick! Hoah!" Her voice is high as she lands back to earth. Now she wants to see how things are going with Hansel. She limps over to the cage and asks him to stick out his tongue. M-m-m-m-m...it looks real tasty. How about his fingers? Here's where Hansel passes the test. He slyly puts out a small bone.

"Giminy...it's like a little stick!" cries the witch.

This will never do. She calls to Gretel.

"Bring raisins and almonds here; Hansel believes he would like some more!"

Now, while the witch is trying to fatten up Hansel, Gretel creeps behind her and takes her wand. She softly tries it out. The witch hears her and quickly turns to ask what it was that she said. Oh, she was just making a wish to Hansel's health! The witch gives her "He-he-he" laugh again and pops a raisin in Gretel's mouth. The fatter the better! Now she goes over to open the oven door. This is what Hansel has been waiting for. He wildly signals to Gretel...and warns her to be careful. He is now out of the cage! In a squeaky voice, the witch gloats over Gretel.

"How my mouth waters for that sweet little child! Come, little Gretel! Little sugar maiden!"

She wants her to take a peek into the oven to see if everything is ready to make gingerbread. Now it's Gretel's turn to pass the test. She decides to act dumb. She wants to know how she will get up there to the door of the oven. It's really quite easy; just lift up and then bend the head. The worried Hansel again warns his little sister to be careful.

"I'm so dumb," shyly admits Gretel.

The witch should show her how to do it. And she does! As the witch, in her cackling way, is bent over the open door, the two children swiftly give her a hefty shove and in she goes! They slam shut the door and chant the witch's song with great delight.

"And when you're inside—bang!
The door shuts—clang!
And *you're* a little roast instead of little Gretel!"

They're overjoyed at their wonderful trick. They fall into each other's arms and then start to dance and sing a happy tune.

"Hurray! Now the wicked witch is dead, dead as a door-nail...and our trouble is over!
Hurray! Now the witch is still, still as a little mouse...,"
their happy voices blend.

Now there are lots of cakes. The witch's dread is over...and so is the spell. So they'll be merry and dance to the light of the fire...and have a wonderful feast! "Hey, hurray, hurray!" their voices end on high.

With that they dance arm in arm to the witch's house. Hansel quickly goes inside and in a moment we see his head sticking out the window. He starts to throw out all kinds of delicious things...while Gretel catches them in her outstretched apron. We hear waltz music and the tinkling of the celeste. But now the oven begins to make loud crackling noises...louder and louder...hotter and hotter it gets until, with one big explosion, it blasts apart! The startled children can't get over it. They rush to the spot and wonder of wonders, they are surrounded by all the boys and girls who were once made of gingerbread! The orchestra gives a chord, the drums roll, then fade.

Gretel looks over the "well-behaved dear children." Hansel wonders how they got there. The strings play softly.

"We're saved, free, for always," sing the motionless children with their eyes closed.

Gretel is amazed that their eyes are shut as if they were sleeping—yet they are singing sweetly. Slowly, the children ask to be touched. Hansel wants *Gretel* to touch them—*he* won't! So she does—one touch on the face of the nearest one. Instantly, his eyes are opened and he gives a big smile, but he cannot move! All the young voices beg to be touched, too! They sound like angels.

So, one by one, Gretel brings them to life. But still none of them move! Hansel gets an idea. He picks up the magic wand and repeats the witch's words he had heard. To make sure it works, he tries a deep voice.

"Hocus, pocus, elderbush!
Disappear, stiff muscles—hush!"

And lo and behold, all the children begin to dance! To a lively, jumpy tune, they all sing. They're so thankful that the witch's spell is gone now that they can sing and dance, happy and free. They form a ring-around and jump and dance...as they think of the marvelous cake they can eat. They want their cheering and their thanks to be heard all through the woods.

Hansel and Gretel, in tuneful duet, remember that the angels of their dreams had predicted it all...that everything would come out all right. So they thank them and praise the angels for "all this glory" which smiles on them. The carefree children, too, join in to thank the angels.

Suddenly, we hear a familiar voice. It is Peter with his "Rallalala!" He wishes that the children were here. (Then Mother and Father come into sight.)

"Ha! Here they are!" he shouts.

"Father! Mother!" cry Hansel and Gretel, running to them.

"Little children!" exclaims Gertrude.

"Here are the poor naughty ones!" cries Peter, as they all fall into each other's arms.

As the strings play along, two boys drag the giant gingerbread witch from the blown-up oven.

In a folk-like melody, Peter tells them all how—through a miracle—the wicked witch became a cake herself—a crunchy-hard cake. The children repeat the same song. Then Peter goes on...

"Notice how heaven punishes:
Evil deeds don't last!
When our need is greatest,
God the Lord is merciful!
Yes, when our need is greatest,
God the Lord holds out his hand!"

His voice ends softly. Then slowly, all repeat his words...getting louder and louder, higher and higher. And as the happy family is circled by the dancing children...the orchestra and bells sing out...on this joyful woodland scene.

THE CURTAIN FALLS

It's not surprising that this bright fairy-tale opera was an immediate success. Children and adults quickly took it to heart, and it was played in over fifty theatres in the very first year. What could be more Christmasy than all those delicious things to eat?...or more seasonal, than Peter's last words: "Yes, when our need is greatest, God...holds out his hand!"

Although Humperdinck created many musical works (including another children's tale called *Konigskinder*—The Royal Children), he will always be famous for his most popular, *Hansel and Gretel*.

Born in Sieburg (near Bonn), Germany, on September 1, 1854, he began studying the piano when he was seven and was writing opera by the age of fourteen! But his folks wanted him to be an architect. (Remember Donizetti?) So off he went to Cologne. That turned out to be a lucky stroke. There, at eighteen, he met Ferdinand Hiller who noticed his talent and took him as his student at the Cologne Conservatory. He stayed four years. (Meanwhile, many of the works he had written by the time he was twenty were destroyed by fire.)

On he went. At twenty-two he won the Mozart scholarship of Frankfurt. Four years later his first works were published. Then he won the Meyerbeer prize, the Mendelssohn prize— and enough money to take a trip to Italy. Of course, here he was luckiest of all—he met Richard Wagner.

Later, while still writing music, he began to teach. . .first as a professor in Spain, then at his own Cologne, then the Hoch Conservatory in Frankfurt. It was at this time that he started to write his famous opera. Three years later, at the age of thirty-nine, he became a world-famous composer.

Many other honors were heaped on him from then on. But, like Mozart, he was never blessed with good health. . .and on September 27, 1921, he died at the age of sixty-seven.

Yet, as with all the great composers we have already met, this brilliant, prize-winning master lives on. *Hansel and Gretel* was first performed in America at Daly's Theatre in New York City on October 8, 1895—just two years after the premiere. Twelve years later, Humperdinck himself came to the Metropolitan to supervise the first production on the afternoon of November 25, 1905. For the next twelve years, it was played there every single Christmastime but one!

Six years later, in 1923, it became the first opera ever to be broadcast in Europe, from London's Covent Garden. And in 1931, on Christmas Day, it had the honor of being the first complete opera ever broadcast from the Metropolitan Opera House.

So, like the gingerbread children, we have come full circle— to a new beginning, and to a happy ending. Our new beginning started with that early opera broadcast—programs that have continued for over fifty years for the enjoyment of millions. Our happy ending has been with *Hansel and Gretel*, which, hopefully, you have enjoyed along with all the other masterwork stories that have been brought to you from the Wonderland of Opera.

APPENDIX

Find the Opera Company Nearest You

UNITED STATES

Alabama
Mobile Opera, Municipal
Theatre

Arizona
Arizona Opera Company,
Tucson

Arkansas
Arkansas Opera Theatre,
Arts Center, Little Rock

California
Opera San Jose, Montgomery
Theater
San Diego Opera
San Francisco Opera
Long Beach Opera, Terrace
Theater

Colorado
Aspen Music Festival, Aspen
Opera Colorado, Boettcher
Hall, Denver

Connecticut
Connecticut Opera, Bushnell
Hall, Hartford
Stamford State Opera,
Stamford Center

Delaware
Opera Delaware, Grand
Opera House, Wilmington

District of Columbia
The Washington Opera, John
F. Kennedy Center,
Washington, D.C.

Florida
Gold Coast Opera, Omni
Auditorium, Pompano
Beach
Greater Miami Opera, Dade
County Auditorium, Miami
Orlando Opera, Bob Carr
Performing Arts Center,
Orlando
Palm Beach Opera, West
Palm Beach Auditorium
Sarasota Opera, Theater of
the Arts, Sarasota
Treasure Coast Opera, St.
Lucy Center, Ft. Pierce

Georgia
Augusta Opera, Imperial
Theatre

Hawaii
Hawaii Opera Theater,
Blaisdell Concert Hall,
Honolulu

Illinois
Chicago Opera Theater,
Athenaeum Theatre,
Chicago

Indiana
Whitewater Opera,
Centerville High School
Auditorium
Indianapolis Opera, Clowes
Memorial Hall

Kentucky
Kentucky Opera, Macauley
Theater, Louisville

Maryland
Baltimore Opera, Lyric Opera
House

Massachusetts
Boston Lyric Opera, Alumni
Auditorium
Opera Company of Boston,
Opera House

Michigan
Michigan Opera Theatre,
Masonic Temple, Detroit
Opera Grand Rapids, De Vos
Hall

Minnesota
Minnesota Opera, St. Paul

Mississippi
Opera South, Mississippi Arts
Center

Missouri
Lyric Opera of Kansas City,
Lyric Theatre
Opera Theatre of St. Louis

Nebraska
Opera Omaha, Orpheum
Theatre

Nevada
Nevada Opera, Pioneer
Theater, Reno

New Mexico
Sante Fe Opera

New Jersey
Metro Lyric Opera,
Paramount Theater, Asbury
Park

Opera Classics of New
Jersey, De Nooyer
Auditorium, Hackensack
New Jersey State Opera,
Symphony Hall, Newark

New York
Caramoor Festival, Katonah
Chautauqua Opera,
Chautauqua
Lake George Opera Festival,
Glens Falls
Metropolitan Opera House,
Lincoln Center
National Grand Opera,
Tilles Center,
C. W. Post Campus, L. I.
New York City Opera, NY
State Theatre, Lincoln
Center
Opera Theatre of Rochester
Syracuse Opera, Crouse-
Hinds Concert Theater
Tri-Cities Opera, The Forum,
Binghamton

North Carolina
Charlotte Opera, Ovens
Auditorium
Piedmont Opera Theater,
Stevens Center,
Winston-Salem

Ohio
Cincinnati Opera, Music Hall
Cleveland Opera, State
Theatre
Opera Columbus, Palace
Theatre
Dayton Opera, Memorial Hall
Toledo Opera, Secor Road

Oklahoma
Tulsa Opera, Chapman Music
Hall

Oregon
Portland Opera, Civic
Auditorium

Pennsylvania
Pennsylvania Opera Theatre,
Walnut Street Theatre,
Philadelphia
Opera Company of
Philadelphia, Academy of
Music
Pittsburgh Opera, Heinz Hall

South Carolina
Spoleto Festival USA,

199

Charleston
Tennessee
Chattanooga Opera, Tivoli
Theatre
Knoxville Opera, Tennessee
Theatre
Opera Memphis, Orpheum
Theatre
Texas
Dallas Opera, Majestic
Theater
Houston Grand Opera, Jones
Hall
Fort Worth Opera
San Antonio Grand Opera
Virginia
Virginia Opera, Norfolk
Center Theatre
Wolf Trap Opera, Trap Road,
Vienna
Washington
Seattle Opera, Opera House
Wisconsin
Florentine Opera, Uihlein
Hall, Milwaukee
Madison Opera, Oscar Mayer
Theatre
Skylight Comic Opera, Pabst
Theatre, Milwaukee

INTERNATIONAL

Argentina
Teatro Colon, Buenos Aires
Australia
Australian Opera, Royal
Exchange, N.S.W.
Austria
Salzburger Festspiele,
Salzburg
Staatsoper, Vienna
Belgium
Opera National, (Rue
Leopold), Brussels
Canada
Calgary Opera, Jubilee
Auditorium
Canadian Opera, O'Keefe
Center, Toronto
Edmonton Opera, Jubilee
Auditorium, Alberta
L'Opera De Montreal, Salle
Wilfrid Pelletier
Opera Hamilton, Great Hall,
Ontario
Manitoba Opera, Centennial
Concert Hall
Ottawa Festival Opera,
Confederation Square,

Ontario
Vancouver Opera, Queen
Elizabeth Theatre
Czechoslovakia
National Theatre, Prague
Denmark
Det Kongeliege Teater,
Copenhagen
Finland
Finnish National Opera,
Helsinki
France
Theatre National de l'Opera,
Place de l'Opera, Paris
Opera du Rhin, Strasbourg
Theatre du Capitale,
Toulouse
Germany (East)
Deutsche Staatsoper, Unter
den Linden, Berlin
Komische Opera,
Behrenstrasse, Berlin
Staatsoper Dresden, Dresden
Stadtisches Theater Leipzig,
Leipzig
Germany (West)
Deutsche Oper Berlin, Berlin
Oper der Stadt Koln, Cologne
Opernhaus Frankfurt,
Frankfurt
Hamburgische Staatsoper,
Hamburg
Bayerische Staatsoper,
Munich
Staatstheater am
Gartnerplatz, Munich
Wurttembergisches
Staatstheater, Stuttgart
Festspielleitung Bayreuth,
Bayreuth
Great Britain
Welsh National Opera, John
Street, Wales
Scottish Opera Limited,
Theatre Royal, Scotland
Glyndebourne Festival Opera,
Sussex
English National Opera,
London Coliseum, London
Royal Opera House, Covent
Garden, London
Hungary
Hungarian State Opera
House, Budapest
Israel
Israel National Opera, Tel
Aviv
Italy
Teatro Comunale, Florence
Teatro alla Scala, Milan

Teatro San Carlo, Naples
Teatro dell' Opera Beniamino
Gigli, Rome
Teatro La Fenice, Venice
Arena di Verona, Verona
Festival of Two Worlds,
Spoleto
Teatro Massimo Bellini,
Catania, Sicily
Politeama Garibaldi, Palermo,
Sicily
Teatro Massimo, Palermo,
Sicily
Monaco
Opera de Monte-Carlo,
Casino, Monte Carlo
Netherlands
Nederlandse Operastichting,
Amsterdam
Norway
Den Norske Opera, Oslo
Poland
Teatr Wielki (Grand
Theatre), Warsaw
Portugal
San Carlos Theatre Opera
House, Lisbon
Russia
Kirov Opera and Ballet
Theatre, Leningrad
Bolshoi Opera, Moscow
Spain
Gran Teatro del Liceo,
Barcelona
Royal Opera House, Madrid
Sweden
Royal Opera, Stockholm
Switzerland
Opernhaus Zurich, Zurich
Grand Theatre de Geneve,
Geneve
Venezuela
Opera Metropolitana, Teatro
Municipal, Caracas
Yugoslavia
Slovensko Narodno
Gledalisce, Ljubljana

OPERA TALK

alto (AHL-toe): The lowest female voice. The same as *contralto*.

aria (AH-ree-ah): An air, melody or song, usually sung by one voice.

barcarole (BAR-cah-role): A rollicking, swaying melody.

baritone: A male voice in the lower range, between tenor and bass.

bass (BASE): The lowest male voice.

basso profondo (BAH-so pro-FOHN-doe): A bass voice that can reach below the lowest bass.

baton (bah-TON): The stick the condutor uses.

bel canto (bell-CAHN-toe): It actually means "beautiful singing." A lyrical style, rather than comic or dramatic.

brasses: The instruments in the orchestra made of brass.

brindisi (BREEN-dee-zee): A drinking song; one of the most famous is in *La Traviata*.

buffa (BOOF-ah): As in opera buffa— comic opera style.

buffo (BOOF-oh): An opera comic like Don Bartolo in *The Barber of Seville*.

cabaletta (cah-bah-LET-tah): A fast song, or part, that reminds one of the beating rhythm of a horse's hooves. From the Spanish *caballo,* meaning horse.

cavatina (cah-vah-TEE-nah): A simple sweet song as sung by Adina in *The Elixir of Love.*

celeste: A musical instrument that gives bell-like tones.

chest tones: Singing tones that come from the chest.

chord: A group of three or more notes played together.

chorus: A group of people who sing all together.

claque (clack): A group of people hired to applaud.

coloratura (cuh-loh-rah-TOOR-ah): A singer, usually female, who sings colorful, flighty, trilling (and thrilling) notes. Violetta in *La Traviata*.

contralto (cohn-TRAHL-toe): The lowest female voice.

crescendo (creh-SHEN-doe): Getting louder.

czardas (CHAR-dahsh): A two-piece Hungarian dance, one slow, one fast. Rosalinda sings a czardas in *Die Fledermaus*.

debut (day-BEW): The first time a singer performs.

diction: A singer or actor who pronounces his/her words so that they can be understood clearly, has good diction.

diminuendo (dee-min-u-EN-doe): When the sound gets softer and softer; either a singer or orchestra.

diva (DEE-vah): It actually translates as "goddess." Used to compliment a woman singer.

discord: When notes that are sung or played are out of harmony.

dramatic: A powerful scene; also applies to voices. Dramatic tenor has a heavier quality than a lyric tenor.

duet: When two singers sing together.

encore (AHN-core): Usually when the audience wants a piece done again, or wants an additional song. It's a compliment.

ensemble (ahn-SOM-bell): When voices or instruments come together as a whole.

entr'acte (AHN-tract): Between the acts (*Carmen*).

fanfare: An announcement, by sound, that something is about to happen. (Horns, drums, etc.)

finale (fee-NAH-leh): The ending.

fioritura (fee-or-ee-TOO-rah): Flowery singing; a lot of beautiful vocal gymnastics.

flat: When a singer hits a note lower than what it's supposed to be.

forte (FOR-tay): Strong, loud.

fortissimo (for-TEES-seemo): Very loudly.

head tones: Singing tones that come from the head.

heldentenor: A strong male voice with trumpet-like top notes and baritone low notes. Usually needed in German operas.

impresario: A manager of an opera company.

intermezzo (in-tehr-METZ-oh): A musical piece usually played between two acts.

legato (leh-GAH-toe): A smooth connection of notes.

leitmotif (LITE-moh-teef): A musical reminder about a character or plot.

librettist (li-BRET-tist): The writer of the words used in an opera.

libretto: The booklet that has the words of an opera.

lyric: A light quality of voice. Also the words of a piece.

lyric bass: A light, rather than a strong, dramatic bass voice.

lyric soprano: A light, rather than a strong, dramatic soprano voice; Adele in *Fledermaus*.

lyric tenor: A light, rather than a strong, dramatic tenor voice. Count Almaviva in *The Barber of Seville*.

madrigal (MAD-ree-gahl): A lyrical love poem.

mezzo-soprano: A female voice lower than a soprano, higher than a contralto.

octave: From one note to eight notes later.

operetta: A light, rather than a grand opera.

orchestration: The way a composer writes down notes for the instruments of the orchestra.

overture: The piece of music that's played before the curtain goes up.

pants role: A part played by a woman dressed as a man. (Prince Orlofsky in *Fledermaus*)

percussion: The instruments that include drums, cymbals, etc.

piano: To play softly; pianissimo, very softly.

pitch: The level of a certain sound. To be "off-pitch" means the sound or tone of the voice (or instrument) is off.

pizzicato (peetz-ee-CAH-toe): Plucking the strings instead of bowing them.

portamento (por-tah-MEN-toe): When a note is carried over to the next line of singing.

prelude: A musical piece that sets the mood for what is to come. The prelude to the third act of *La Traviata*.

premiere: An opera's first performance.

prima donna: A female singer who is a star; actually means "first lady." Sometimes it refers to a singer who is hard to get along with.

prologue: The part that's performed before the opera really starts; it explains things ahead of time, as in *Romeo et Juliette*. (Not every opera has a prologue.)

prompter: The person who feeds the performers their lines so they won't forget. (Unfortunately, he can sometimes be heard too.)

props: The little things that help a scene—books, candles, vases, etc.

proscenium (proe-SEEN-ee-uhm): The arch that frames the stage.

quartet: Four voices singing or four instruments playing. (The famous quartet at the end of *Rigoletto*)

quintet: Five (see quartet).

range: The distance between low notes and high notes that can be reached by a voice.

recitativo (reh-chee-tah-TEE-voh): Words that are more spoken than sung.

refrain: A melody that's sometimes repeated.

repertory: The different operas that a company will perform.

score: The parts that are written for voices and instruments.

septet: Seven (see quartet).

set: The scene where the action takes place.

sextet: Six (see quartet). The famous one is from Donizetti's *Lucia di Lammermoor.*

singspiel (ZING-shpeel): A work with sung as well as spoken words.

solo: Alone.

soprano: Highest female voice.

sotto voce (SOHT-toh VOH-cheh): "Under-voice"; secretive.

spinto: A voice that goes beyond what is expected.

staccato (stah-CAH-toe): Usually rapid, separate notes; opposite of legato.

strings: Violins, violas—instruments played with a bow.

tarantella (tare-an-TELL-lah): A rapid, whirling folk dance.

tempo: The "time" or pace of music.

tenor: Highest male voice.

tessitura (tehs-ee-TOOR-ah): When a piece has a lot of high notes that a singer is required to reach.

transpose: When music is written higher or lower than the original.

tremolo: A "wavering" of the voice that has to be done very carefully.

trill: A "quivering" of the voice between two notes.

trio: Three.

verismo (vehr-EEZ-moe): True-to-life opera.

vibrato (vih-BRAH-toe): A "vibrating" of the voice that needs to be done carefully.

vocalize: When a singer practices.

winds: Instruments that are blown through: oboe, clarinet, brasses etc.

woodwinds: Instruments that may be made of wood or metal: flute, piccolo, bassoon, oboe, clarinet.

SELECT BIBLIOGRAPHY OF COMPOSERS

JOHANN STRAUSS

Fantel, Hans. *The Waltz Kings*. New York: Wm. Morrow and Co., 1972.

Jacob, H. E. *Johann Strauss*. New York: The Greystone Press, 1940.

CHARLES GOUNOD

Cross, Milton. *Encyclopedia of the Great Composers and Their Music*. New York: Doubleday and Co., 1953.

The New Grove Dictionary of Music and Musicians. Vol. 7. New York: St. Martin's Press, 1954.

GIOACHINO ROSSINI

Toye, Francis. *Rossini: A Study in Tragicomedy*. New York: Alfred A. Knopf, 1947.

Toye, Francis. *Rossini*. London: Arthur Backer, 1954.

Weinstock, Herbert. *Rossini*. New York: Alfred A. Knopf, 1968.

GEORGES BIZET

Cooper, Martin. *Georges Bizet*. London: Oxford University Press, 1938.

Curtiss, Mina. *Bizet and His World*. New York: Alfred A. Knopf, 1958.

Dean, Winton. *Georges Bizet*. London: Cambridge University Press, 1948.

GIUSEPPE VERDI

Baldini, Gabriele. *The Story of Giuseppe Verdi*. New York: Cambridge University Press, 1980.

Bonavia, Ferruccio. *Verdi*. London: Dobson Books, 1947.

de Schauensee, Max. *The Collector's Verdi and Puccini*. New York: J. A. Lippincott Co., 1978.

Martin, George. *Verdi, His Music, Life and Times*. New York: Dodd, Mead and Co., 1963.

Shean, Vincent. *Orpheus at Eighty*. New York: Random House, 1958.

Toye, Francis. *Giuseppe Verdi, His Life and Works*. New York: Alfred A. Knopf, 1946.

Walker, Frank. *The Man Verdi*. New York: Alfred A. Knopf, 1962.

Ybarra, T. R. *Verdi: Miracle Man of Opera*. New York: Harcourt, Brace and Co., 1955.

GIACOMO PUCCINI

Greenfeld, Howard. *Puccini*. New York: G. P. Putnam and Sons, 1980.

Jackson, Stanley. *Monsieur Butterfly*. Briarcliff Manor, New York: Stein and Day, Scarborough House, 1974.

Marek, George R. *Puccini: A Biography*. New York: Simon and Schuster, 1951.

Mosco and Carner. *Puccini: A Critical Biography*. New York: Alfred A. Knopf, 1959.

GAETANO DONIZETTI

Ashbrook, William. *Donizetti and His Operas*. New York: Cambridge University Press, 1982.

Weinstock, Herbert. *Gaetano Donizetti*. New York: Pantheon Books, 1963.

RICHARD WAGNER

Chancellor, John. *Wagner*. Boston: Little, Brown & Co., 1978.

Gal, Hans. *Richard Wagner*. Briar Cliff Manor, New York: Stein and Day, Scarborough House, 1963.

Gutman, Robert W. *Richard Wagner, the Man, His Mind and His Music*. New York: Harcourt, Brace and World, Inc., 1968.

Gregor-Dellin, Martin. *Richard Wagner, His Life, His Work, His Century*. (2nd Volume). New York: Harcourt, Brace, and Jovanovich, 1983.

Newman, Ernest. *The Life of Richard Wagner*. 4 vols. New York: Alfred A. Knopf, 1933-1946.

WOLFGANG AMADEUS MOZART

Burk, John N. *Mozart and His Music*. New York: Random House, 1959.

Einstein, Alfred. *Mozart: His Character, His Work*. New York: Oxford University Press, 1945.

Turner, W. J. *Mozart: The Man and His Works*. New York: Alfred A. Knopf, 1938.

ENGLEBERT HUMPERDINCK

The New Grove Dictionary of Music and Musicians. Vol. 8, 6th ed. Edited by Stanley Sadie. New York: Grove Dictionaries of Music, Inc., 1980.

PROPER NAME INDEX